How to Get Loose From a Snapping Turtle - Before It Thunders...

HOW TO GET LOOSE FROM A SNAPPING

TURTLE - BEFORE IT THUNDERS...

and hundreds of other amazing (and sometimes unusual) homespun remedies, cures, and "fixes"

JAMES L. COTTON, JR.

The diversity of brand names and products referenced at various places in this
book, and hereinafter specifically listed, are registered trademarks: Alberta VO5,
Carfax, Consumer Reports, Crisco, Endust, Heinz 57, Pam, Peppy Les Peu,
Pepto-Bismol, 7-Up, Sprite and WD-40.

This book was printed in the United States of America.

To order additional copies of this book, contact:
Xlibris Corporation
1-888-795-4274
www.Xlibris.com
Orders@Xlibris.com
16982

"'Tis well to borrow from the good and great;
'Tis wise to learn; 'tis god-like to create."
—J.G. Saxe

Important Notice

ACKNOWLEDGEMENTS

Although I am identified as the sole author, innumerable persons have contributed to this work; first, to the Appalachian people whose innovative ideas and remarkable knack for common sense solutions inspired this book, I extend my deepest gratitude. Special acknowledgement is made to my parents, James and Carolyn Cotton, who gave me such a wonderful childhood chocked full of mountain wit, wisdom and wonder. Also, to my loyal secretary and friend, Lou Ann Smith, who patiently converted my legal pad-scribblings to the typewritten word. And, finally, to my wife Lisa and children, Caroline and Luke; without their immeasurable love and support, this book would not have been possible.

James L. Cotton, Jr.
Graperough Road
Oneida, Tennessee

PREFACE

Since my boyhood, I have been intrigued by the natural talent and knack of mountain folks, for good old-fashioned "horse sense".

Having a good childhood, is surely one of life's sweetest blessings. My early youth in the mountains of East Tennessee was filled with fishing, hunting, camping, Boy Scouts, a wide variety of part-time jobs, and wonderful, involved parents. In later years, it was filled with a decade's worth of summers in Western North Carolina climbing mountains, canoeing rivers, and trekking sections of the Appalachian Trail. It was at the edge of a mountain lake at Camp Ridgecrest in North Carolina, that I really did learn how to get loose from a snapping turtle—but that's another story.

In the years between the educational pursuits of college and law school, I learned more of life's subtle but important lessons in coal mining work, and from working in the family business. My father is a master woodworker who refinishes and restores antiques, and my mother has had a lifelong love affair with folk art and antiques.

All of this gave me the opportunity, over the years, to meet and learn from a diverse and fascinating group of Appalachian people. Often, I was able to catch some of their **"homespun remedies, cures and fixes"** in the net of these experiences.

So, long ago, I began keeping a private journal of these little gems of common sense that I had heard of, or learned from these folks. I reduced to writing as many as I could remember from childhood memories, fearing they would be forever lost. Almost twenty-five years of practicing law, with more than a decade of them on the bench as a judge, has given me a unique vantage point and education into the remarkable ability of mountain people to concoct innovative solutions and remedies, where at first blush, none are apparent.

Only a handful of the ideas in this book are purely my own. Mostly, they are the contributions of family, friends and interesting people I have known and met through the years – homemakers, quiltmakers, physicians, lawyers and lawmen; mechanics, master craftsmen and scoutmasters; photographers, preachers, teachers, and backwoods philosophers; coal miners, coon hunters, car salesmen and carpenters; florists, farmers, fishermen and courthouse "fixtures". Some of the contributors were mountain people with advanced degrees in higher learning. Some were common folks who had very little formal "learnin" – but had "PhD's" in common sense.

The compilation of "**homespun remedies, cures and fixes**" contained in this book are not, by any stretch of the imagination, of profound importance or literary significance. But they are imaginative and inexpensive cures to everyday problems that simply make life go a little easier and dollars a little farther – and hopefully, are just fun to read. This, from a larger perspective, reflects the simple, yet enlightened philosophy of Appalachian people in curing life's little problems, that says " . . . for every pound of learning, a person needs 10 pounds of common sense to apply it."

Sincerely,
James L. Cotton, Jr.

CONTENTS

SECRET TO KEEP YOUR LOAF OF BREAD AND COOKIES FRESH . . . LONGER

To keep bread fresh for a longer period of time, place a stalk of celery in the bread bag. Place half an apple in with your sealed container of cookies or cake, and these baked goodies will stay fresh. When you purchase extra loaves of bread to freeze, place a clean (preferably washed with bleach), white wash cloth or dish towel in each bread bag before sticking them in the freezer – this cloth will pull out the moisture and keep the bread firm. Bonus Tip: To soften up lumpy, hardened brown sugar, make sure it's in an airtight container, and place two slices of fresh bread with it, for two days.

Nifty Use Of 35 Millimeter Film And "Other" Containers

Save your 35 millimeter film containers – they make great storage for needles, buttons, paper clips, small screws and the sort. If you have a friend that is a nurse or lab technician, or can order for a medical supply house, obtain some urine specimen containers (unused, of course!). These strong, transparent containers, with screw-on lids and outside labels for marking, are super storage for nuts and bolts, small nails and screws, and other tiny items that need to be saved, protected and easily marked for identification.

Some Acupressure For Headaches And Leg Cramps

For many folks, headaches and other minor pain can be relieved by firmly squeezing, for about a couple of minutes at varying intervals, on one of the main acupressure points which is located on the stretch of skin attached between the thumb and forefinger. Following a jog, or a day of yard work or hiking, many people get leg cramps, even after going to bed. For quick relief from most leg cramps, firmly grip the upper lip between your thumb and index finger, and squeeze for about a minute.

WORLD'S BEST TIP FOR GAS GRILL USERS

It's a common problem – how to clean your gas grill rack and briquettes, from all those food and grease drippings. The secret to easy gas grill cleaning: place aluminum foil, shiny side down, so that it covers the entire grill plate surface. Close the grill lid. Turn grill on "high" heat, and leave it for 10-20 minutes, depending on the extent of food and grease build-up. Once the grill completely cools, you'll find the food and grease deposits on your grill places and briquettes baked into a ash-like coating, which can be easily brushed off with a grill brush.

How To Know How Much Paint Is In The Can – Without Opening It

Before resealing and storing away your paint can, attach a piece of duct or masking tape, or mark a line on the outside to identify the remaining paint level – next time, you'll know exactly how much paint is left, without pulling it off the top shelf or opening the can. Bonus Tip: A piece of masking tape stretched across an opened paint can, makes an excellent "striker", to wipe excess paint from a dipped brush. Never load more than one-half of a paintbrush with paint, when dipping it, for best control and results.

A QUICK AND EASY ICE PACK

Look in your freezer. A pack of frozen peas or giblet corn, which will fit nicely to body contours, make an excellent ice pack for your aches and pains. Wrap the pack with a thin towel or other cloth covering, to prevent ice burn to the skin.

A Bar Of Soap Can Do More Than Clean

Here are some valuable uses for a bar of soap: 1. Rub around the sides of a screw with a bar of soap, and it will install into the wood much easier. 2. Rub soap in a stuck zipper mechanism to work it loose, and on the full length of the zipper itself to keep it working smoothly. 3. Rub a bar of soap along the bottom runners of the drawers in your furniture when they stick, to restore the glide.

BEST HOMEMADE ALL-PURPOSE CLEANER EVER MADE

Mix together:

(1) ½ gallon (2 quarts) of warm water
(2) 1 cup of white vinegar
(3) 2 cups of ammonia
(4) ½ cup of baking soda

This time-tested cleaner can be just as effective as expensive store brands, disinfects, contains no harsh chemicals and costs only pennies! Use in spray bottles for convenience. **Warning**—don't mix bleach with this formula – it could create dangerous vapors.

Antibiotics Can Discolor Gold Jewelry

If you are taking a pretty heavy or extended dosage of antibiotics, you may want to remove gold rings or other valuable gold jewelry, until you stop taking the medication and it clears your system. Why? It may ruin it. Antibiotics can sometimes cause gold to discolor.

How To Restore Stickiness To Old Tape

If you have an old roll of masking tape or electrical tape that is loosing its stickiness, don't throw it away. Place the roll in the microwave, and run on high about 10–15 seconds, or so. This will often restore the tape's adhesive qualities.

A BACK-UP REMEDY FOR SHAVING NICKS

Next time you start the day with a nick from your razor, and you don't have any of the usual stinging antiseptic to stop bleeding – grab your stick of lip balm, and give it a smear. It works, and doesn't even burn!

Use Stale Bread To Clean Your Photos

When your photographs are covered with dust or oily fingerprints, clean them with a slice of stale bread (don't use the "ends"). Stale bread absorbs the dust and oil, and acts as a mild but safe abrasive to clean the face of the photo. By the way, if you want to write on the back of a photo, purchase an inexpensive pack of file labels at your office supply store, and write on them. Then stick the label on the back of the photo. Why? Any writing in ink made directly on the back of a photo will eventually bleed through and ruin it. Bonus Tip: Stale bread also works well, to remove greasy finger prints from cloth book covers; you can also use baking soda or cornstarch on cloth book covers to absorb the oil from fingerprints, let it sit overnight, and then gently brush off the next day.

Don't Make The Antifreeze Mistake

More is not always better, especially with chemical mixtures. When directions call for one cup, it's human nature to mistakenly think two cups will be twice as effective. For example, some people, during harsh winters, use pure antifreeze in their radiator figuring if antifreeze mixed with water per manufacturer's directions protects to –30 below, then pure antifreeze won't freeze at all. Wrong. Pure antifreeze freezes solid, at temperatures just below zero. Moral of story – always carefully follow directions when using any chemicals.

How To Avoid "Loud" Clothing In The Woods

If silently moving through the woods is essential to the success of your hunting or wildlife observations, remember that wool, besides being one of the most durable clothing materials, is about the only material that doesn't make that "sandpaper" sound, when your legs rub together or your sleeves rub against the jacket. Frontiersmen and early settlers knew this well—it was the difference in surviving and starvation.

Neat Way To Avoid Messy Paint Can Lids

With a hammer and nail, or with your power drill, place several holes in the groove of the top rim of the paint can. This will allow paint to drain back down into the can and avoid the squishy mess that comes with refastening the lid. Bonus Tip: The second coat of paint requires one-third less paint, than needed for the first coat. By the way, rather than use two coats of high-dollar, expensive brand of paint, consider this alternative—use a less expensive brand of paint for your primer and first coat.

"Baby's Bottom" Cure For Dry, Chapped Hands

For dry, chapped hands, apply diaper rash ointment – it really works! If you really want to get a jump start on the healing process for badly chapped hands, try this home remedy that's been around for many years; generously apply and rub in your hand treatment crème or ointment right before going to bed, and immediately put on a pair of clean, cotton gloves for the entire night. Next morning, you'll already notice the improvement.

GREAT USES FOR OLD GARDEN HOSE

Before throwing out your old garden hose, remember that it has other great uses. 1. Cut off the length needed for your handle, and splice it with a cut down its entire length. Then attach it to your bucket handles (wrap it with some duct tape, to secure the hose), and you have it – a durable and padded bucket handle, especially handy for carrying heavy loads. 2. Hose spliced in this fashion, also makes a good storage cover when wrapped around circular saw blades. 3. To clean out your vacuum hose, cut a section of old garden hose that is about one foot longer than your vacuum hose. Use this piece to run through your vacuum hose – it's just wide enough to effectively clear debris and flexible enough to easily work back and forth through the vacuum hose.

Baby Oil Great For Chrome

To clean and get a super shine on chrome faucets and other chrome-trim fixtures around the house, using a soft polishing cloth, rub them down with a dab of baby oil. What a shine!

SECRET FOR EASY CLEANING OF BALL CAPS

Place your soiled baseball cap so that it's wedged among the prongs of the rack of your automatic dishwasher – it'll come out slightly damp and fresh as a daisy! Remember to shape it up while damp, and then let it finish air drying.

How To Prevent Your Bathroom Mirror From Fogging

Wipe your bathroom mirror with regular shaving cream (not the "gel" type), and then wipe off and buff with a cotton cloth or towel. This will prevent your mirror from fogging up. Works great on diving masks too! Bonus Tip: your hairdryer will de-fog your bathroom mirror in only seconds.

HOMEMADE REMEDIES FOR STINGS THAT REALLY WORK

One of the best treatments for stings such as bees, wasps, yellow jackets and hornets is meat tenderizer. Honeybees leave their barbed stinger in you (most other stinging insects don't), so first remove the stinger, preferably by "scraping" off the stinger rather than "pulling" out the stinger which can squeeze the venom sac attached to the stinger and inject more venom into the sting. Remarkably, the venom sac on a honeybees dislodged stinger can continue to pump its venom into you for several minutes, so get it out of there! Wash off all stings with soap and water to remove bacteria. Then mix the tenderizer with water to create a thick paste, and generously apply it to the sting area. The secret to quick relief from stings—is to treat quickly. The faster this paste or other remedy is applied (preferably within three minutes of the sting), the better the relief. As an alternative to meat tenderizer, some folks' get quick relief from the throbbing with a drop or two of ammonia. For those not allergic to aspirin, many get pain relief from wetting the sting area and rubbing plain aspirin on it. Using an ice pack can bring instant relief. Of course, if there is an unusual or adverse reaction to a sting, immediately seek professional medical treatment. Bonus Tip: Watch out about swatting yellow jackets. When smashed, yellow jackets give off a chemical alarm which alerts the other yellow jackets in the area to attack and sting!

How To Charm Your Chain Saw

Anyone who has operated a chain saw, knows the hassles of keeping the cutting chain oiled, which must be frequently done while you're cutting wood. Even with the "self lubricating" chains, you must constantly add oil directly to the chain, to keep it working effectively. There's a simple way to eliminate this hassle. Purchase a plastic squeeze bottle with an easy-open top, or use an old plastic shampoo bottle with a large flip-up opening, and fill it with your chain oil. Then, as the chain on your chain saw needs oil, just grab the bottle and squeeze! Bonus Tip: Splitting logs with an axe can be pretty dangerous, especially when the split wood flies off through the air, or a glancing blow deflects the axe towards your leg. There's an old logger's trick to reduce this danger—stack up two old tires on top of each other, and split wood inside the tires. This ring of tires will often block-flying wood, and absorb the miss-hits or the glancing blows of your axe.

Binoculars Double As Back-Up Magnifying Glass

If camping or at home, you find yourself in dire need of a magnifying glass to remove a splinter or repair a tiny object – use your binoculars. Look through the "wrong end" of the binoculars, locating the viewed object next to the eyepiece end, and adjust to the magnification you need.

To Recover From Diarrhea – Call On The "Brat"

To overcome the cramping, hunger and misery of diarrhea, careful attention must be given to what you eat. At first, "clear" foods and drinks like Jell-O, chicken broth and tea are the best place to start. If this goes well, many physicians recommend you quickly move up to the "BRAT" diet regimen, which is an acronym for Bananas, Rice, Applesauce and Toast. This simple guide really works. Of course, if diarrhea persists without recovery, immediately seek professional medical treatment.

How To Bring Stealth To Your Fishing Or Wildlife Observation Boat

This one comes out of the "old fisherman's" bag of tricks. Save old carpet and lay it in the floor of your fishing boat or canoe, so you can quietly move around without alerting the fish below. You can also glue carpet on the bottom of tackle boxes, coolers and other containers for extra "stealthy" movements. This is a good trip for wildlife observers as well. Bonus Tip: If you like observing wildlife from a canoe or rowboat, you can eliminate the noise that results from the throat of the canoe paddle or oars bumping and rubbing against the side of the boat, with each stroke of the paddle or oar. Buy a tube of foam pipe insulation from your building supply store. It only costs a dollar or so, it's durable, and already split down the side. All you have to do is cut the length needed (it usually comes in 6 ft. lengths), and fasten it over the edges (sometimes called "gunwales") of the canoe or boat. You may want to cover both sides of the entire boat, so you'll have extra pieces on hand if one gets damaged or lost.

Neat Trick For Cleaning Up A Broken Egg

Next time you drop a raw egg on the kitchen floor or counter, sift salt over the broken egg. The salt changes the consistency of the egg, making it very easy to wipe up. Bonus Tip: Don't be fooled by the hard shell on eggs – they absorb refrigerator odors all the same. The flavor of eggs will remain best, if kept in a covered, snapped-tight container – not in the open egg tray conveniently featured in every fridge.

Easy Removal Of That Stubborn Bumper Sticker or Decal

Although some vinyl bumper stickers will easily peel off, many bumper stickers and glass decals, especially if they're made of paper or been baked on the bumper or glass for many years, can be extremely difficult to scrape off or remove. Solution: generously soak the bumper sticker or decal with "mineral spirits" (not paint thinner; they're not the same) and let it soak a few minutes. Even the toughest and stickiest bumper sticker or decal will easily rub off, with no scraping or scuffed knuckles. When using mineral spirits on glass, follow up with a rub of alcohol or glass cleaner to remove the oily residue that mineral spirits can leave on glass. To remove the dealer's raised logo, heat the area with a blow dryer, slowly and carefully working the blade of a putty knife under the logo to pry it off. Use mineral spirits to remove any remaining residue. To protect your car's finish, fold a piece of duct tape over the putty knife blade.

HOT TIP TO INCREASE THE BURN-TIME OF CANDLES

Place candles in the refrigerator a few hours before using them – they'll burn much longer! Bonus tips: To easily remove candle wax from metal candleholders, place them in the freezer overnight, and the next day you can just break and peel off the wax with your fingers, or by scraping with the edge of a plastic spoon. To get wax drippings from your tablecloth, put a clean, highly-absorbent cloth on top of the wax, and set a hot iron on it. Most of the wax will be melted by the iron, and be drawn up into the cloth. Touch up, if necessary, with a cleaning product. This works on most carpets too!

How To Avoid Overloading A Canoe

As a result of several summers of using canoes on rivers and lakes, we had a "rule-of-thumb" for inexperienced canoeist, to make sure they never overloaded a canoe. The rule: after the canoe is fully loaded with people and supplies, there should never be less than 7 to 8 inches of canoe exposed directly above the water line as measured at the center of mid-line point of the outside of the canoe. Although the application of this rule-of-thumb can vary with canoe style and size, and an experienced canoeist can safely transport more weight than allowed by the limits of this rule, it does for most types of canoes, provide novices and families with a simple and reliable test to assure safe loading of their canoe. No matter what, always strictly follow the load and weight guidelines of the canoe manufacturer. Bonus Tip: Proper storage is the secret to extending the life of your canoe. How? Keep your canoe out of the sun, dry, off the ground, covered with a breathable tarp and upside down, resting on a rack or sawhorses with its weight equally placed on its opposite gunnels or "gunwales".

Simple Way To Clean A Tough Casserole Dish

A generous dose of automatic dishwasher detergent placed in a casserole or desert dish, filled with hot water, stirred and soaking for 30 minutes, makes cleaning the dish too easy to believe.

The Secret For Changing A Tire On Rugged Roads

If you ever have a flat tire on a rugged back road or ground, where the surface is so uneven there's not enough room to slide your jack underneath the vehicle, the ground is too hard to dig out a hole or recess for the base of the jack, and there's no help in sight or other alternatives—try this swift little trick: Lay your spare on the ground, placed right in front of the flat tire being changed. Pull your vehicle forward, so that the flat tire comes to rest on top of the spare. Then insert your jack (you now have plenty of room) and lift the vehicle so that it clears the spare tire. Pull the spare off the ground, and change the flat. You're out of there!

HOW TO MAKE CHEAP DAMP-WIPES FOR BABY BAG OR TRAVEL

Fold individual paper towel sheets into fourths, making as many as you need. Wet the paper towels, and place them in zip-seal plastic bag. To really improve these homemade wipes, mix 1-2 tablespoons of a "baby wash" product with a couple of tall glasses of water (experiment with the "scent strength" you prefer), for soaking your paper towels – this will give them a pleasant aroma, preferable to expensive store versions. For further convenience, you can cut a paper towel roll in half (a serrated knife works best), soak the "half roll" in the baby-wash mixture, remove excess water and the cardboard roll in the center, and then place the half-roll in a zip-seal plastic bag or even better, a closely fitting, air-tight plastic container. This allows you to tear-off one or more wipes at a time, as needed. Use good quality paper towels when you make these homemade wipes.

Removing Chewing Gum From Hair and Carpet (Without Scissors!)

My mother always reached for the jar of peanut butter, when one of the children got chewing gum in their hair. Work the peanut butter into the entangled gum, and it combs right out. By the way, you can place a couple of ice cubes in a small plastic bag, and hold them over the chewing gum and make it easy to remove (you can remove chewing gum from carpet using the same "ice" technique.)Bonus Tip: Peanut butter also works well in removing lipstick stains – just make sure and wash the stained fabric before the peanut butter dries.

World's Best Tip For Storing Strands Of Christmas Lights

Next Christmas season, pick up from your hardware store or home center a few of the plastic, H-shaped holders that are used for storing extension cords. These devices are inexpensive, and make it very easy to access, wrap-up and store strands of Christmas lights—they even have a clip for locking the plug into place.

Handy Tip For Cleaning Greasy Hands

To clean oil or grease off of hands and avoid the expense of costly hand-cleaner products, scrub hands with a generous portion of Crisco. Wipe hands with a dry rag, and follow-up with a soapy wash. Works on tree sap too! If you have just an occasional engine repair, oil change or other greasy task, a simple solution is to keep a box of rubber surgical gloves "on hand". They don't interfere with any type of detail work, and when the job is over, you just peel them off and throw away. Bonus Tip: A coat of hairdressing cream on the hands, like Alberta VO5, applied before painting or greasy work begins, makes the hands easy to clean at the end of the job.

The Secrets Of Buying Comfortable Shoes

Someone once said, "we spend the least money on the two things we spend the most time on – our shoes and mattresses". Here's a few "insider" secrets from the trade, to getting a good fit: 1. Try on shoes towards the end of the day, when your feet are largest. 2. Always leave a finger's width of space between your longest toe and the front of your shoes. 3. Make sure there is no gap of space between your ankle and the shoe while walking. 4. Buy shoes only by the "fit" – not by the size on the box; shoe sizes significantly vary between styles, shapes and brand. 5. It's common for people to have one foot larger than the other; buy shoes to fit the larger foot. 6 . Test the fit of your shoes while standing up, and then walk in them. 7. Only buy shoes that are comfortable when you try them on and while walking in them. 8. Don't buy snug or tight shoes, counting on them to stretch – they don't.

A FEW SIMPLE WAYS TO REDUCE COMPUTER OR READING EYESTRAIN

To significantly reduce eyestrain from staring at your computer, or from reading fatigue: (1) About every 10-15 minutes just take a moment to look away from your computer screen (or book), and focus for only a few seconds on an object at least 30 feet in distance from you; (2) About every hour, stand up and stretch, and then look out a window to visually track with your eyes (without moving your head) the varying heights and shapes of the skyline buildings or horizon (mountains, trees, etc.). No window? Then trace with your eyes the shapes of the walls of your room, finishing up with the eye exercise of looking up and down, then side to side, without moving your head; (3) Frequently close your eyes for a few seconds to break-up the fixed glare of computer work, to prevent eyes from drying out; (4) Eliminate white paper from lying around the computer screen.

CORNMEAL CAN RELIEVE CHAFFING FOR WALKERS AND HIKERS

I learned from hiking on sections of the Appalachian Trail in the mountains of Tennessee and North Carolina, that walking for extended distances can cause the skin between your legs to badly chafe. Baby or talcum powder, which most folks reach for first, are actually ineffective, because they have a tendency to cake up on the skin. While on the Trail, an old friend passed along his "magic" remedy to me . . . cornstarch! Cornstarch works amazingly well for chafed skin – the moisture in the chafed area turns the cornstarch into a soothing lubricant; later, after the long walk, hike or jog is over, you can treat the chafed area at home with the proper pharmacy product.

Simple Way To Cover Human Scent When Observing Or Hunting Deer

According to experienced deer hunters and wild life observers, it's not always easy to stay upwind of deer. Changing wind direction can suddenly give you away and spook the deer. Some deer observers and hunters stick a couple of ripe apples in their jacket or pants pockets, knowing that deer love apples. The aroma of these apples sometimes keep the deer hanging around in their vicinity, and also helps to cover the human scent. Makes a nice snack, too.

Great Way To Clean Your Electric Can Opener

The blades of electric can openers often contain food residue from opened cans, which can be a dangerous harbor for bacteria. A great way to clean your electric can opener is to generously spray some bleach or antibacterial cleaner on a folded paper towel, and then feed the saturated, folded edge of the paper towel through the cutting blade on the opener. This will remove stubborn food build-up from the blade and disinfect it at the same time.

HOW TO GET CRAYON MARKS FROM FURNITURE

To get crayon marks out of wood furniture, generously rub mayonnaise into marks, and let it soak for about 15 minutes. Then rub clean with a damp cotton cloth. Bonus Tip: A crayon of the same color, or sometimes even better, one a shade darker than the wood being repaired, makes an excellent repair stick for touching-up and filling in scratches on wood furniture. Softening the crayon with a blow dryer or match flame, just before application, can really help if filling dents.

HOMEMADE REMEDIES TO KEEP DEER OUT OF PLANTS

Deer are magnificent creatures to observe, but they can do heavy damage by eating and stomping on gardens and flowers. For a cheap, effective and harmless deer repellent, mix 4 teaspoons of dishwashing liquid, 4 teaspoons of red hot pepper sauce and 4 eggs (good use for outdated or spoiled eggs!) per gallon of water. Apply as frequently as needed with a garden sprayer to areas being protected. Deer are repulsed by this smell, which is not detectable by humans. Human hair (check with a barber at the end of his day), balled-up the size of an orange and tied off in a nylon stocking and hung from a shrub or tree, provide lingering human scent and will often keep deer away from that area. Or you can stretch a taut fishing line around the perimeter of your plants, about 32 inches high, which will spook deer to run, when they unexpectedly bump it. Also, deer hate to walk on chicken-wire, placed flat on the ground. Bonus Tip: Trouble with squirrels in your attic or garage loft? Sprinkle a cheap strong-smelling perfume around their hangout – they probably won't be back.

Homemade Way To Clean Your Automatic Dishwasher

To clean and freshen-up the inside of your automatic dishwasher, first empty the dishwasher of all items. Snugly fit two cups of white vinegar on the bottom rack. Then spread half a box of baking soda over the bottom of the dishwasher. Run the dishwasher through the wash and rinse cycles, but shut the dishwasher off before it runs through the drying cycle (or place on setting that skips the "dry" cycle). Now it's sparkling clean and odor free!

Don't Butter Up Your Burns

It is just as important to know the homemade remedies that don't work – as those that do. For minor burns, don't use butter. This "old timey" remedy will only lead to infection. Don't use ice, despite the old wives' tale that it helps – freezing cold will kill skin cells, just like the burn. So, what's the answer? Immediately cool the burn with cold water, or with a compress made of a clean washcloth or paper towel soaked with cold water (if you can't get the burn under the faucet). Act quickly – the cold water helps most, when applied immediately after the burn, by eliminating the skin-damaging heat.

World's Best Homemade All-Purpose Drain Opener

(1) 1 cup of white vinegar
(2) 2 cups of salt
(3) 2 cups of baking soda

Mix these ingredients together, and pour them down your clogged drain. In about 30 minutes, pour at least a gallon of boiling water down the drain. This will likely clear the clog, contains no harsh or dangerous chemicals to harm the pipes or the user – and is cheap! Bonus Tip: Don't pour this mixture on top of clogged commercial drain openers – it could create hazardous vapors, or cause an explosive reaction that shoots out dangerous chemicals in your face.

How To Keep Drawers And Chests Smelling Fresh

Cut up your favorite aroma of deodorant soap into 3 or 4 blocks, best wrapped and tied off in cheesecloth or a piece of old pantyhose, and put them in your clothes drawers or chests. They will keep the clothes smelling fresh, moth-proof and cost much less than dried flower sachets which soon crumble and loose their scent. Bonus Tip: Deodorant soap, wrapped in the same way, makes a great pincushion – and gives a wonderful fragrance to your sewing box!

Sticky Trick For Working With Dried Flowers

When rearranging your dried flower arrangement, spray it with a good, sticky hairspray – it will prevent many of the fragile berries, petals and grasses from breaking off as you work.

Homemade Remedy For Dry or Callused Feet

For joggers, those constantly on their feet and many folks during the winter months—dry, scaly and irritated feet are a common problem. The cure? Before you go to bed, rub down your feet with petroleum jelly, and put on some white cotton socks. Next morning, the problem will be dramatically improved or gone! If you suffer from planter's warts or tough calluses on your feet, soak your feet for 30 minutes for 30 consecutive days in white vinegar, and at the end of this treatment, the planter's warts and calluses will be greatly relieved.

How To Prevent And Remove Rings In Your Bathtub – And Get Soft Skin Too

To prevent "ring around the tub" and soften your skin, add 2-3 tablespoons of baking soda to your bath water. Already got a ring in the tub? Out of expensive household cleaning chemicals? No problem – grab your shampoo and pour it in a sponge or rag. The ring of dirt or bath oil easily wipes off.

Best Way To Dry Wet Athletic Shoes Or Boots

Next time you've washed or are otherwise stuck with a wet pair of athletic shoes, place them overnight up against the heat exhaust located next to the floor at the bottom of the front door of your refrigerator. For wet leather shoes or boots, rotate their position every 2-3 hours in front of the warm air, including laying them on their side so warm air flows inside the shoes or boots. This method works like a commercial shoe or boot dryer, which slowly dries the footwear. Drying footwear by setting them on a heater or using a blow dryer will dry the shoes or boots too quickly, causing the leather to become uncomfortably stiff and even crack. Bonus Tip: If a refrigerator is not handy, stuffing wet shoes or boots with crumpled-up newspaper (black & white print only), left in over-night, will remove most of the dampness; if you're camping, warm, dry sawdust (removed and replaced every 3-4 hours) works very well.

How To Get Rid Of Dryer Lint On Clothes

Toss a pair of old panty hose or two into the dryer with your wet clothes, at the start of the drying cycle. Lint will cling to the panty hose – not your clothes.

How To Make An Inexpensive Workshop Dust Filter

If you're tackling a woodworking job that will be generating a lot of fine wood dust and particles, in addition to wearing a mask, you can inexpensively remove much of the airborne dust and particles from your workshop by attaching an inexpensive central air or furnace filter to the intake side of a box fan (you can use duct tape to attach the filter), so that air is drawn into the fan through the filter. For best results, position the fan so it is near the worksite where dust is created, or so that air is drawn out of the workshop towards the exterior of the building. They cost a little more, but you can purchase filters that are specifically-designed for trapping small dust particles. Bonus Tip: Hang a shoebag in your workshop—the shoe pockets make handy storage places for your spray can products.

A Rinse Solution To Extend The Life Of Your Washer

To keep your washer free from bacteria, mold and the build-up of residue from detergents and fabric softeners, every two or three months, run 1 quart of white vinegar and 1 cup of ammonia through the hot wash cycle (of course, with no clothes in it). This will extend the life of your washer.

CURING THE COMMON PROBLEM OF FEISTY EYEGLASS SCREWS

If a screw in the frames of your eyeglasses continues to work itself loose, coat the screw with clear nail polish, let it dry, and screw it back in. Chances are, this will cure this problem. If you lose the screw, often a stud earring, used in place of the screw, will temporarily hold the eyeglasses and earpiece together. By the way, for less than two bucks, you can get an eyeglass screwdriver. This miniature tool is indispensable for those wearing glasses – and it works much better than a knife blade, nail clippers or fingernail! When working with eyeglass screws, or other small objects, place them on the sticky side of a piece of tape – you won't lose them! Bonus tips: Tear off a piece of newspaper (black and white print only) and use it to clean your eyeglass lens; its cheap, handy and effective. However, use a very soft cloth for softer plastic lenses. An equal-parts mixture of white vinegar and water makes an excellent cleaning solution, which you can keep ready-to-go in a small spray bottle. Never use commercial glass cleaner which can melt away the protective coating placed on glass and plastic lenses.

Secret To Making Really-Comfortable Broom & Mop Handles

Pick up a tube of pipe insulation at your building supply store for about a buck. It's made of durable foam, split down the side so it is easy to wrap around the pipe, and typically comes in 6 ft. lengths which may have to be shortened a bit to fit the handle. Apply an all-purpose glue to the wooden handle of your broom or mop, and attach the tube of insulation. This will provide a soft and comfortable, easy-grip handle, that will also reduce fatigue.

Some Uses For Used Fabric Softener Sheets – That May Surprise You

Save your used fabric softener sheets from the dryer, stuff them in a zip-lock bag, and keep them under the sink. 1. Next time you have a tough-to-clean desert or casserole dish, put a couple of these sheets in the dish, fill it with hot water and let it soak overnight. Next morning, it will easily wipe clean. 2. Used fabric softener sheets can be repeat performers by placing them in the rinse cycle of your wash loads. 3. Used fabric softener sheets make a good buffing cloth for windows (don't use newspapers – they leave behind paper residue) and for stainless steel sinks (don't use them on shiny *chrome* – they're too abrasive!). To remove soap and water spots from stainless steel, rub down with white vinegar, rinse and then buff with fabric softener sheets.

Good Tip For Finding Wind Direction On A Calm Day

Wildlife observers and hunters know the importance of selecting an observation point that is upwind, so animals are not alerted. If you need to know wind direction on a calm or mildly windy day, strike a match, blow it out and stick it into the ground. Another way is to take a burning stick from your campfire, blow it out, and push it in the ground. The trail of smoke will give you a reliable read on wind direction.

"Clean" Trick For Fishing Things Out Of The Toilet

When a child's toy, one of your cosmetics or other item falls in the toilet, avoid the unpleasant and challenging task of fishing out the item with a couple of pencils. The simple and sanitary solution: Turn a plastic trash bag inside out, put your hand down in it, and reach into the toilet bowl to pick up the item. Then lift out the item, pull the bag back over the item and tie it off, for a trip to the trash. And you never even touched the water! Bonus Tip: Save your plastic grocery bags (that don't leak!), stuff them in a paper towel tube and stick it under the bathroom sink, so you're ready for this one.

Secrets For Catching Fishing Worms

Here are some valuable secrets I learned as a boy, for catching a mess of fishing worms, sometimes called "worm fishing". Fill a bucket with hot water, adding about one handful of powdered clothes detergent or ¼ cup of liquid clothes detergent in it. Some folks add a "dab" (i.e., a tablespoon) of ammonia or white vinegar to this, but don't overdo it. Pour this mixture over the ground in the area where night crawlers or worms are located. The worms will climb out to the top of the ground in only a few minutes. Rinse the worms off with fresh water, before packing them for your fishing trip, to extend their life. Another method of worm fishing is to drive a metal or wooden stake firmly in the ground where worms are located. With a hammer, bang on the top of the stake at an angle (not directly down on the top) or against its side, or rub across the stake with another similar stake in a motion imitating a bow across a fiddle—the vibrations will flush out the worms to the top of the ground. Bonus Tip: When hunting worms on top of the ground at night, cover your flashlight lens with a sheet of red or yellow cellophane, fastening it on with a rubber band. Why? Worms will quickly turn back down into their holes when the white light of your flashlight hits them, but the soft light through the cellophane does not spook the worms nearly as much.

The Secret To Cleaning Football Uniforms And Really Grubby Clothes

Getting grass-stained football uniforms or construction work clothes clean again, is no easy chore – until now. Here's the secret: Add and stir up 1 cup of automatic dishwasher detergent and 1 cup of liquid clothes detergent to your washer, then load the clothes. Let them soak overnight, and then run them through the full wash cycle. Game time!

How To Make A Wonderful Homemade Air Freshener

To make a good-smelling, natural air freshener for your closet, vanity or bathroom, stick whole cloves (stem first) into an apple leaving the head of the cloves resting snugly on top of and against the outside skin of the apple, until it is completely covered with cloves. Then wrap the apple with some attractive, mesh material from your cloth shop, selecting a color you like. Tie off the ball of material surrounding the apple with a strand of decorative ribbon which is used to hang the apple. The wonderful fragrance will last for weeks. This makes a great craft project for the kids! Bonus Tip: Whole cloves repel moths better than smelly moth balls, and when they are wrapped in cheesecloth and made into a sachet, keep clothes drawers moth-free and provide a wonderful fragrance among your clothes.

Prevent Glue Container-Caps from Being "Glued"

To avoid the cap of your glue or caulking tube from sticking to the container, wipe some petroleum jelly around the threads where the cap fits. Bonus tips: When using wood glue to fasten wood pieces (especially where wooden legs, spindles, rungs or other pieces are being inserted and glued into a slot or hollow sleeve), mixing a small amount of sawdust in with the glue by stirring the mixture on cardboard or other smooth disposable surface, will strengthen the glued assembly. Remember – for maximum "hold", use glues only in the range of room temperature (65 deg. F – 80 deg. F).

The Secrets To Predicting A Dog's Personality

Some of the "old timers" in our mountain region who have enjoyed a close bond and companionship with their dogs, use methods passed down through the years to give them a prediction on the personality of a dog. Whether a purebred or a "Heinz 57", they try to determine if the puppy is one of three basic personality types: a **strong personality** with dominant characteristics; a **normal personality** with more balanced behavior; or a **weak personality** with submissive characteristics. One method is to place a puppy in their lap, lying on its back, while the holder consoles and calms it. A puppy with a "strong" personality will continue struggling. A "normal" personality will initially resist and struggle a little, then soon begin to settle down. A "weak" personality will be passive or lethargic, and may even panic or shiver with fright. Another method is to hold a puppy so its feet are 3 or 4 inches above the ground or floor. A "strong" will keep on struggling. A "normal" will struggle some, then eventually calm down. A "weak" will just dangle there like a rag doll with little resistance. One technique often used by sportsmen who are looking for a good hunting dog or just a spirited canine companion, is to put a puppy on the ground or floor, and throw it a small play object. They're looking for a puppy with a "strong" personality that motivates it to run after and play with the object – not a puppy that carries the object away, is disinterested, or appears to be frightened.

HOME REMEDY TO AVOID TRAVELING DIARRHEA

If you are one of those adult persons who suffer the merciless wrath of diarrhea brought on by travel, whether journeying in other countries, or on extensive trips or vacations. You may want to try this remedy: take two tablespoons of Pepto-Bismol 5-6 times a day, at equal and regular intervals, starting 2-3 days before the trip begins and continuing without interruption through a couple of days after the trip is over. Of course, carefully read and follow the directions and warnings on the Pepto-Bismol label.

A Ringer Of An Idea To Carry And Store Horseshoes

Pitching horseshoes is great fun, but carrying horseshoes around, or finding a good way to store them, is a problem. The perfect answer for this problem sometimes reveals itself at flea markets and yard sales – a bowling ball bag!

Good Foods From Your Home – For Houseplants

These are good foods to mix in the soil for healthy houseplants: 1. Diced banana peels. 2. Ground-up egg shells. 3. One pack of unflavored gelatin dissolved in a quart of water. By the way, ferns like a strong cup of tea.

How To Discourage Obscene Telephone Calls

Tuck away, next to your telephone, a referee's whistle or one of those super-shrill security whistles you can blow when about to be attacked. If you get a random obscene telephone call, stick the whistle in the telephone mouthpiece and let it rip! They'll get "the message." However, if you get multiple calls from the same person or voice, immediately contact your local district attorney's office and police department; with your cooperation, they can likely trace the source.

How To Freshen Up Plastic Food Containers

For convenient and healthy food storage, its hard to top plastic storage containers. However, spiced-up leftovers like lasagna, chili and soups leave a lingering smell in the container long after it has made several trips through the dishwasher. What to do? Crumple up newspaper (black & white print only), stuff it in the container, and seal it off with a burp. After 24 hours has passed, open the container and remove the paper – smell is gone! Bonus Tip: If your container is stained, fill it with water and add ½ cup of bleach. Let is soak overnight. Pour out the water-bleach mixture, giving it a final scrub with some of your automatic dishwasher detergent. If a stain or smell persists, mix up a paste of white vinegar and baking soda, and generously coat the stain. Replace the container lid and let the container set a few hours. Scrub out the paste and rinse thoroughly. This should eliminate most of the stain.

SECRET OF KEEPING FRESH FLOWERS . . . FRESH LONGER

To keep fresh flowers looking good, do the following: 1. Frequently cut off stem ends. When you trim the stems, make a clean cut (don't break or tear the stems), cut the bottoms at a 45 degree angle, and cut a 1-2 inch slit up the side of the stem – this will help the flowers to "drink" more. 2. Add a couple of tablespoons of clear soft drink, like 7-Up or Sprite (not diet!), and an aspirin per small vase. A good recipe is two cans of clear soda and four aspirins per gallon of water. Also, 2-3 drops of bleach alone, per vase, works well. 3. Use warm water in your vase – not hot or cold. 4. Avoid putting flowers in direct sunlight. 5. Don't allow blooms or leaves, on the lower section of the flower stem, to remain submerged in the water – cut them off. Bonus Tip: Fresh cut daffodils bleed a milky fluid that close-off the cut stem, which keeps the stems from "drinking" its water; to remedy this problem, pass the end of the cut stems, for only a moment, through a flame. Another Bonus Tip: Got weeds around your flowers? The "claw" end of a good ol'fashioned claw hammer makes a super tool for digging up weeds, deep roots and all!

THE MYTH ABOUT FURNITURE POLISH

Polish is fine for dusting. But I learned from my father, who is a master at refinishing and repairing wood, that the common belief you can enrich or "feed the wood" on fine furniture with polish – is just a myth. Dad explains that if wood has been properly finished and sealed by varnish, paint, polyurethane or lacquer, there can be no "feeding the wood," because polish cannot penetrate through the finish into the wood grain. His recommendation is simple, cheap and effective: rub the wood furnishing with a soft, cotton cloth, lightly coated with mineral spirits (not paint thinner!). Looks great!

Homemade Remedies For Hiccups

Next attack of the hiccups try one or more of these old reliable cures: 1. Dry-swallow a teaspoon of sugar, or a healthy glob of peanut butter. 2. Pull with force on your tongue. 3. Bend over forward with the top of your head pointing to the floor (as much as possible) and drink a glass of water in this "upside down" fashion, keeping your mouth below the glass while drinking. 4. Breathe into a paper bag. 5. Gargle water while holding your breath. 6. Try to sneeze or cough (you can induce a sneeze by sniffing pepper or vinegar). 7. Hold your breath as long as you can.

Easy Way To Clean And Rust-Proof Garden Tools

Keeping yard and garden tools clean and also oiled to prevent their corrosion, is a time-consuming chore. To simplify this task, fill a bucket with sand. Next pour oil (used motor oil from your car works great) into the bucket and mix. Now, when your tools get caked with dirt, work them around in the sand bucket, which will both clean them and leave an oil residue to stop rust. This method is really handy during the busy growing season, if you have a garden that you work in every day or so. Bonus Tip: Measure and mark a lineal "yardstick" on the blade and handles of your shovel or post-hole digger—you'll know the depth of your hole, as you dig!

How To Stay Alive In Forest Used For Both Recreation And Hunting

In many parts of our country, as in mine, hikers and campers share forests with those that hunt the whitetail deer and other game having white spots on them. As a boy, I learned the "unwritten" hunters code to avoid being mistakenly shot, that every hiker, camper and hunter should know where forests are used both for recreational and hunting use: (1) Don't carry or use white handkerchiefs, or any white clothing (the exposure of white underwear, if "nature calls", can be a dangerous moment!); (2) Don't carry branches of wood on your shoulder for your campfire (could be mistaken as antlers); and (3) Don't expose or fold white socks over the top of your boots. Most importantly, wear orange. Some people make the mistake of wearing bright red, thinking it will protect them – it won't. Why? Red looks black from the distance –orange doesn't.

Slick Trick To Keep Ice Cubes From Sticking To Your Ice Machine Tray

To prevent ice cubes from sticking to your ice machine catch-tray, clean the tray with dishwashing detergent and dry. Then spray the tray interior with a light coating of a non-stick food spray, like Pam. Wipe the excess. The food spray will not taint the taste of the ice, and will last for weeks.

SLICK TRICK FOR INSTALLING WOOD SCREWS

Rub a bar of soap around the threads of the screw, and it will be much easier to install – and much less likely to split the wood! Bonus Tip: Rub a bar of soap along the bottom runners of the drawers in your furniture when they stick, to instantly restore the glide.

A Simple Procedure To Save Jewelry And Contact Lenses

When putting on or removing jewelry or contact lenses in front of the mirror located behind your sink, always lay a towel in the belly of the sink so that the towel, not the drain, catches the fumble.

How To Keep Ants Out Of Picnic Food

If you're camping or on a picnic, and it becomes difficult to keep ants out of your food, try this old logger's trick: Soak baling twine or a heavy string in kerosene (or in a strong insecticide or bug repellent), set your food up on a stump or rock, and then wrap the kerosene-soaked twine or string around the stump or rock. Ants won't cross it! You can prepare this string, and place it in a "freezer" quality zip-lock bag, so you can safely travel with it to the picnic site.

A Back-Up Knife Sharpener You Didn't Think Of

There's truth in the old adage, that "dull knives are more dangerous than sharp ones." Accidents really are more likely to occur with dull knives. For a make-shift knife sharpener, use the rough bottom of a ceramic vase or cup. Pull the knife blade across the bottom rim in the same way you would use a sharpening stone. Bonus Tip: If you need to sharpen a craft knife, box knife blade or edge of a small item, the striking-surface on a matchbox can provide a good substitute for a sharpening stone.

THE SMART AND SAFE WAY TO STORE A LADDER

Storing a ladder can be a real problem. Left on the floor—it gets in the way. Leaning unfastened against the wall—it's unsafe. Here's the perfect solution: Have a leather shop make a belt-shaped strap, about 2 inches wide and 20 inches long, with a heavy duty snap inserted so the ends fasten together; make a paper template for a trial run on your ladder size. Attach this strap to the wall in your storage room (have the leather shop install a grommet for the attachment screw) at the height of the top step. Now stand your ladder against the wall, wrap and snap the strap around the top step and presto – your ladder is safely and conveniently stored! Another strap can be added at the bottom step, to double-secure the ladder. Bonus Tip: An old belt, attached in this fashion, works just as well.

An Amazing Device For Lighting Hard-To-Reach Pilot Lights

Have trouble reaching the pilot light on your furnace or fireplace with a match? Make the perfect tool for this job by crimping or gluing an alligator clip (they're cheap – get one from your local hardware store) on the end of a broken-off antenna from an old radio, walkie-talkies or car. This creates a telescoping device to hold your burning match, that will easily reach even the most recessed pilot lights. This device also works great as a safe way to light charcoal and gas cooking grills, or fireworks on the Fourth of July!

Temporary Relief For Lost Tooth Filling

Filling the space left in a tooth from a lost filling with the softened wax from a birthday candle, can bring significant relief from pain until you can get to the dentist. Bonus Tip: if you are on the unfortunate scene where a child or someone has a tooth knocked completely out, do not pick up the tooth by its root (make sure to handle it only by the crown), rinse it off with milk, if available, and if possible, place it back in its socket, heading immediately to the dentist office. If the tooth cannot be put back in its socket, store it in milk and rush straight to the dentist.

Keep Bugs Out Of The Flour And Sugar

To keep bugs and insects out of your sugar and flour bins, add one or two bay leaves to them. Here's one from our old school cafeteria: Place a few grains of raw rice in your salt shakers, to prevent the salt from forming clumps. Bonus Tip: To keep silverfish out of bathroom drawers, sink cabinets and other places without using toxic insect repellants, sprinkle a little cinnamon where they're spotted.

If Ever Lost In The Woods – This Could Help

When people are lost or disoriented in the woods, they have a tendency to travel in circles. Once you have determined a direction you want to travel (by climbing a tree to spot a destination or landmark, using a compass, etc.), use the technique of spotting a tree or other object that is straight ahead in the same direction, and travel to it. Continue this technique, going from point to point – it can prevent miles of aimless wandering around and around in large circles, wasting precious energy and daylight time. This method has helped save me on several occasions, when lost in the thick undergrowth of Appalachian mountain country. Most importantly, don't panic or run. Breathe deeply, relax and tell yourself you'll be okay, because you will. Smoke from a campfire (make sure its safe!) is the easiest for rescuers to spot.

A Home For Lost Socks

Around our home, we joke about the "land of the lost socks" – it's truly a mystery, how single socks disappear during the wash and dry cycle, leaving an aggravating pile of unmatched socks. After weeks of looking at a single sock, we finally throw it away only to have its mate suddenly appear in the next laundry load. A simple solution: hang a small cotton or mesh bag with a drawstring (they're very inexpensive) on a wall inside your closet, as a temporary home for orphan socks. Sooner or later, the prodigal sock will show up, for a happy reunion on your feet.

Quick & Easy Way To Lubricate Door Hinges

Spray a non-stick food spray in door hinges to lubricate and eliminate squeaks, and to lubricate window and door tracks, all without the "oily" smell of petroleum products. However, don't use food spray on lock mechanisms – graphite products are much better.

World's Best (And Cheapest!) Disposable Makeup Removers

Makeup is difficult, and sometimes impossible, to remove from washcloths. Baby wipes are great as disposable wipes for removing makeup, for home and travel. Buy the cheap generic brands, which work just as well. They even make baby wipes containing aloe!

A Simple and Easy Way To Clean Your Microwave

Today, most heating and cooking of food is done in the microwave, leaving the inside covered with the usual spills and splashes of baked-on food. There's a simple way to prime your microwave for easy cleaning. Boil a large cup of water in the microwave for about five minutes – this softens the spills and splashes, so that it is easy to wipe clean, and avoids the need for abrasive cleaners or scrub pads that are harmful to the microwave interior. To freshen-up your microwave, boil a large cup of water containing 2-3 tablespoons of lemon juice in your microwave for five minutes. Bonus Tip: To prevent this build-up on the inside of your microwave, regularly give the interior panels a wipe with a solution made of equal parts of white vinegar and water – works great!

THE MIRACLE OF MINERAL SPIRITS

Mineral spirits (not to be confused with paint thinner!) is an amazing and versatile product. It is flammable, so be careful how you use it and where you store it. Among other things, it works great for: 1. Removing stubborn scuff marks and stains from wood floors covered with polyurethane. 2. Removing price stickers, glued-on labels and glue residue from products, without scraping or damage. 3. Wonder how a wood surface will look if you placed a clear varnish finish on it? Rub a light coating of mineral spirits on the wood, and you'll know! 4. To keep a skin from forming on top of your oil-based cans of paint, even during months of storage, before you reseal the can, put some mineral spirits in a spray bottle and mist-spray only about a teaspoon (or less) of mineral spirits on top of the paint. Replace the lid. Be careful not to drop, shake or agitate the paint can while storing it.

The Secret Of Easy Oven Cleaning

Before tackling the tough job of cleaning baked-on grease in your oven, soften up the chore and prepare the oven as follows: Turn the oven on its lowest or "warm" setting for 15 minutes, then cut it off. Next, put a cup of ammonia in a small glass bowl on the upper rack, and a large metal pan of boiling water on the bottom rack. Don't open the oven for at least 12 hours. When you do, the oven should easily wipe clean, without harsh fumes or chemicals. Use a scrub brush and baking soda on any tough spots that might be left. Wipe off the inside of the oven with a good rinse of water. Bonus Tip: Although lining the bottom of your oven with aluminum foil or pan is a nice way to avoid scrubbing and keep your oven drip free – its not worth it. The aluminum foil or pan disrupts and hampers the effective flow of convection heat, resulting in an oven that heats food unevenly and inconsistently.

How To Revive Dying Minnows In Your Bucket

If you notice that some of the minnows in your bucket are starting to turn belly up and float to the top, before you lose them all, drop 1 or 2 plain aspirins in your minnow bucket. This will likely revive your minnows for a few more hours.

The Secret Of Using Plastic Under A Home As Moisture Barrier

It's well known that moisture trapped underneath the floors of a home can, in short time, do serious damage and cost thousands of dollars to repair. A commonly-used and effective method in eliminating dampness under a home is placing plastic on the ground below the subfloors, to create a "moisture barrier". Warning: covering all of the ground underneath the home with plastic will totally seal off ground moisture, but in turn, could choke off the home from proper ventilation or "breathing", which actually creates another source of moisture from the "sweating" that occurs. To avoid this problem, don't cover all of the ground underneath the home with plastic – cover only about 80% of the ground, by leaving 2-3 feet of bare "breathing" ground next to all exterior walls of the home.

Keep Moisture In – Cats Out Of Indoor Plants

Pine cones (the fresher, the better), when placed on top of the soil of indoor plants, will help to trap moisture in the soil and will even deter inquisitive cats from digging in the pot. Also, a bed of pine needles or moss are other good ways to maintain moisture in the soil of indoor plants.

Homemade Remedy For Motion Sickness

For generations, folks in our mountain area knew that chewing on a piece of candied ginger could often relieve indigestion or nausea. Ginger can still work wonders with an upset stomach or motion sickness – sailors from the Far East knew this, even centuries ago. For motion sickness, add one-quarter teaspoon of salt to a glass of a gingerale product (use a gingerale drink that actually contains "ginger", and not a substitute flavoring). Drink this concoction while it is still vigorously fizzing. Or, you can take about 1 teaspoon of powdered ginger (or a one 1000 milligram capsule for your health food store), about 30 minutes before boating or travel, and another such dose every 3-4 hours thereafter if still traveling, which for many folks can be very effective at preventing or curbing motion sickness.

Old Farm Trick For Baiting A Mousetrap

When baiting a mousetrap, use pumpkin seeds – mice can't resist them. Leaving a little of the pumpkin pulp mixed with the seeds won't hurt. After Halloween, keep some of this irresistible mouse bait for the rest of the year, by storing pumpkin seed and pulp in an airtight container. Keep it in the refrigerator, or freeze for it long-duration storage. Bonus Tip: If no pumpkin pulp is available, use peanut butter with a drop of syrup on top – it's equally irresistible to mice!

A Math Secret Our Third Grade Teacher Didn't Tell Us

Remember how tough it was in 3rd grade to memorize the multiplication tables for the "9's"? There's a little secret, to know if your "9 times" are correct. When multiplying the 9's, if your multiplication answer is correct, the two numbers making up the answer will always add up to 9! Examples: 9 x 7 = 63 (i.e., 6 + 3 = 9). 9 x 4 = 36 (i.e., 3 + 6 = 9). If only Jethro Bodine had known.

How To Reduce Clogging Underneath Your Mower

With the engine off, spray the clean bottom of your lawn mower with a good coat of non-stick food spray – grass will not so readily stick and clog, and after mowing, it will be easier to spray off and clean. Bonus Tip: Spray non-stick food spray on your snow shovel, to keep snow and ice from sticking to it and bogging you down. Use of petroleum-based lubricants on your snow shovel can ruin clothing and stain your concrete drive.

Surprising Secret For Stopping A Nosebleed

Contrary to our natural instincts, often the best way to stop a routine nosebleed, remarkably enough, is to give your nose one good, healthy blow, before applying any pressure. This removes any accumulated blood clots, that can wedge open the bleeding vessels. Of course, if a nosebleed continues without responding to ordinary courses of treatment, immediately consult your physician.

NUMBER ONE PLUMBER'S TIP

Each week, pour a pot of boiling water down the drain of your sinks, showers and tubs (not the toilet – it could damage it!). All plumbers agree this cheap, simple and environmentally-safe procedure is the best preventative maintenance there is to avoid clogged drains. Bonus Tip: avoid use of bleach and other harsh chemicals in your drains and garbage disposal systems, especially if they are hooked up to a septic tank. Bleach and other chemicals kill the natural organisms that keep your septic system unclogged and working. Use only organically safe and compatible products to pour into your septic system.

Nice Tip On When To Avoid Oil As A Lubricant

Although oil is an excellent and universally-known lubricant, it's not the only type of lubricant or always the best one for a particular job. For example, avoid using oil and oil-based spray lubricants in door and other locking mechanisms. Oil lubricants attract and accumulate dust and dirt, which will eventually obstruct the smooth operation of the lock and even wear it out. Instead, use the lesser-known "graphite" lubricants that come in powdered form, and in easy-to-use dispensers so it can be squeezed into small openings. Graphite doesn't collect dust and dirt, and is the best for locks and hinges. Anytime dust and dirt can get to the mechanisms being lubricated, use graphite instead of oil, unless the manufacturer specifies otherwise.

How To Remove Oil And Grease From Concrete

Concrete driveways and garage floors inevitably get grease and oil stains. Many cleaning chemicals just don't work, and very strong chemicals like muriatic acid are expensive, dangerous to use, remove the protective sealer on the concrete, and can even dissolve a blemish into the concrete itself. Another alternative? Pour a cooking pot of very hot water, containing a couple of tablespoons of dishwashing detergent and ammonia, dropping directly on the stain to flush out the oil, and repeating as needed. It will remove most of the stain; however – don't pour boiling or very hot water on concrete that is cold or below freezing, which can cause cracking. The sooner you do this after the oil or grease gets on the concrete, the more effective this method will be. *Use extreme caution* with the hot water! If you want to avoid the risks of handling very hot water, for a very fresh oil spill, you can generously cover it with cornmeal or baking soda, and about 30 minutes later, sweep away much of the oil with a broom. For extra tough stains, after using the baking soda step to remove excess oil, mix up a thick mixture of dishwashing detergent and baking soda, working it into the stain and letting it soak about an hour. Then add some salt, some hydrogen peroxide and scrub with a stiff brush, rinsing thoroughly. Bonus Tip: A homemade concrete sealer can be made out of equal parts of kerosene and boiled linseed oil (don't boil kerosene—it's highly flammable!); brush it on and let it fully dry. Another Bonus Tip: If you have weeds growing in or around your concrete walks, or around brick or stone walkways, boiling hot water is a great environmentally safe weed-killer – and cheap!

Old Trick For Those Who Enjoy Worm Fishing

With all the hi-tech gadgetry available in the fishing industry today, sometimes the most fun, especially with children, is to relax on the bank with a cane pole or simple rod & reel, and fish with worms. A nice trick, used by old timers, is to pack the worm in a tight ball of mud, and then lower it into the water. The dissolving mud catches the attention of vicinity fish, and is a "presentation" (as the pro's call it!) too tempting for the fish to resist!

How To Spot (Not Stain) An Authentic Oriental Rug

Years of experience are essential in evaluating the weaves and value of exotic rugs and tapestries, but if you're a person who enjoys sifting through flea market and garage sale rugs, hoping to find that "buy of a lifetime" Oriental, there's a quick test I learned from my mother, who has a very good eye for antique linens and rugs, to know if the rug is likely authentic and handcrafted. The test: Spread apart the pile on the rug. If there are knots at the bottom of the pile, then the rug is truly handmade. No knots? Then it's made by machine. Don't be fooled by sewn-on fringes, they're usually a sure sign of a machine-made rug.

Forget-Proof Record Of Paint Colors In Your House

When we painted all of the rooms and ceiling of our house, we used about a dozen different colors. We made a list of these colors and their mixture formulas, but likely won't be able to find it in a few years, when we need it. Here's a sure way to keep a reliable and convenient record of your paint colors: Remove the cover plate on the light switch nearest the entrance door (this routine helps to know which switch plate, among several in a room, that you color-coded). On a self-adhesive file label or masking tape, write the name, brand and mix formula for paint used in that room, stick it inside the cover plate, and reattach to the wall. Forget proof!

Best Single Photography Tip Ever for Amateurs

Cameras now do all the focusing for you – the challenge is catching the good moment on film. I recently heard one of the most famous photographers in America reveal on TV their simple secret for getting wonderful photos of children. The professional's advice: Always keep the camera on an open shelf in a place of quick and easy access, loaded with film and ready to shoot. Posed photo sessions often end up with the usual mugging for the camera, and when you spot a great, unscripted moment, by the time you find, load and return with the camera, you've already lost the precious opportunity. In short – be able to instantly grab and shoot. Those ordinary scenes of children covered with Mom's make-up, wearing Dad's big hat and shoes or intensely lecturing the puppy, that can never be staged, suddenly, when captured on film in unposed and spontaneous settings, enable us amateurs to take amazingly good photographs.

How To Make Homemade Plaster To Repair Walls

To create a homemade filler for small cracks or nail holes in your sheetrock or plaster walls, mix up a thick batch of white glue and baking soda, and then fill the cracks with a putty knife. Bonus Tip: A plunger makes a great container to mix and hold plaster, as you work with it to make small repairs.

Plastic Milk Jugs Make Great Paint Containers

Use plastic juice or milk jugs to store opened latex paint – their sure grip handle, with two or three marbles or ball-bearings dropped inside, make a handy, easy-to-stir container. Bonus Tip: As a young Boy Scout camping out near rivers or lakes, we used empty milk and bleach plastic jugs to mark off our designated safe area for swimming, by anchoring the corner jugs to the bottom with rope and rocks, and then by tying together the rest of the jugs with nylon rope to form the perimeters. Still works!

Homemade Remedies To Fight Poison Ivy Itch

Very few itches can rival poison ivy. There are some old, but effective remedies for poison ivy itch that have been passed down for generations: (1) Make a thick paste out of baking soda and water, and apply it to the rash; (2) Apply an ice pack (packages of frozen peas or corn nicely conform to body shapes and work well) to the rash – it will provide temporary, but fast relief from itching; (3) Put a cup of colloidal oatmeal (colloidal oatmeal has been ground to a fine powder to keep it dissolved in water), available from your pharmacy, in a clean, white athletic sock, tie it off, and let the sock soak in 2-3 cups of cool water for about 10 minutes. Then remove the sock, and dab it directly on the rash. (4) If the poison ivy is all over the person, soak in a cool bath of water containing 2-3 cups of "colloidal" oatmeal; (5) Apply cool slices of cucumber to the rash, for instant and soothing relief. This is quite soothing for sunburn, too; (6) A moistened tea bag, applied directly to the rash, brings relief; (7) One of the most soothing treatments is to apply a gauze compress of ice-cold, whole milk (not skim) on the rash; rinse so you won't turn "sour". Of course, if poison ivy becomes severe, or does not steadily improve, immediately consult your physician.

Great Tip For "Prepping" A Paint Roller

Before painting with a new roller, wrap it with packing or duct tape, and then peel. This will remove the small clumps of roller material that can interfere with a smooth and even coat of paint. Bonus Tip: Line your paint tray with aluminum foil – it's easy to clean (just throw out the foil) and allows permanent use of the tray.

Secret For Pumping Life Into Your Minnows

As a boy, we significantly extended the life of our minnows, by using our bicycle pump and pumping about a minute's worth of air into the minnow bucket, about three times an hour. Today, you can do this more easily and often, with an air pump that plugs in the accessory switch of your vehicle.

How To Clean Dirty Oven Racks

Cleaning the tough, baked-on grease from oven racks is a real hassle and messy job. Next-time, try this "no scrub – no mess" formula: Mix a solution of 2 cups of ammonia, 1 cup of automatic dishwasher detergent and 1 gallon of water. Go outside (in case of a leak) and place the racks in a heavy-duty strength plastic bag. Pour this solution over the racks into the bag and tightly seal off the bag, leaving the bag for 12-24 hours. Later, the racks should easily clean with a steel brush. Rinse them off thoroughly.

Cedar Chests Can Be Hazardous To Quilts

Yes – cedar chests are off limits to moths, but don't pack your heirloom homemade quilts in a cedar chest, without one more protective step. Quilts, or any other linens or cloth materials, will permanently discolor and be damaged in only a few months from making direct contact with cedar wood. Cedar wood has sulfur in it! Roll up (don't fold – this avoids permanent creases) your quilts or linens, and completely wrap them in acid-free tissue paper before putting them in the cedar chest, which will extend and preserve their condition for years. For maximum protection, re-wrap with fresh acid-free paper every 3 years. A good coat of polyurethane on the inside walls of the cedar chest will also protect its contents. Bonus Tip: Don't wrap your quilts and linens in plastic bags as a substitute for acid-free paper; this will also discolor and ruin them. Another bonus: If through the years your cedar chest has lost that good cedar aroma, just sand the inside of it with a fine grade sandpaper (sand only with the grain), and that good cedar smell will come back like new!

World's Best Homemade Odor-Remover For Refrigerator

To make a super filter to remove the food odors from your refrigerator or freezer, fill up a coffee can with activated charcoal or cat litter. Then punch the plastic lid full of pencil-size holes and snap it back on. Place this homemade filter in the fridge or freezer, routinely stirring the contents for maximum effect. Another good freshener for your refrigerator is imitation vanilla extract (not pure vanilla flavoring), placed in an open container.

How To Make A Cheap, But Very Good Chamois Cloth

Save your old sweatshirts and sweatpants. When cut up and turned inside-out, they make great buffing cloths for rubbing down your car and other things needing a soft touch. Bonus Tip: hang on to old panty hose, too. Not only do they make excellent paint strainers, but they also put a great shine on freshly polished shoes.

The Handy But Unknown Guide In Every Home To Know What Size Objects Can Choke A Child

With small children or grandchildren in your home, you can never be too vigilant in keeping tiny toys, broken pieces of toys, or other small items out of their little hands and mouths, that can choke them. Even some fast food toys are dangerous for children under the age of three. Parents hear a drumbeat of warnings and guidelines (such as "no item smaller than a half-dollar"), but have no reliable, on-the-spot template to go by. A failsafe device for determining if an item is too small for children under age three, surprising enough, is in every home. It's the tube inside a standard toilet paper roll! If any item, by both its length and width, will pass into and fit inside the opening rim of a toilet paper tube, its too dangerous for a small child.

Nice Homemade Fix For Tears In Leather

There's a quick, easy cosmetic fix for a hole or tear in smooth leather (not suede) furniture. Using a lighter or match, melt the end of a crayon, of matching color, and let it drip into the damaged area. Then rub the site with your finger, to get a smooth, blended finish. For tears, it can help to first prepared the damaged place with a little glue, or by gluing a piece of support leather or vinyl underneath the tear flaps – then apply the crayon. This process can sometimes work on the thicker vinyl materials (be careful not to melt or damage thinner vinyls with the hot crayon). Bonus Tip: a shot of hairspray will remove fresh stains from smooth leather. For tougher stains, apply a good lather of old fashioned "saddle soap", or use petroleum jelly which can be left on a while to soak-up and absorb the stain, and later wiped off.

The Secret To "Swat" Dust Under The Refrigerator

Stretch a sock over your fly swatter, and spray it with some Endust. It's a great way to clean under your refrigerator, or the tight spot between cabinets or appliances.

Ladies—How To Eliminate Static-Cling Between Skirt And Slip

To eliminate your skirt from sticking to and climbing up your slip, rub a metal coat hanger over the inside of the skirt and the slip – the coat hanger will absorb the static "electricity". This will also work to remove static from your hair. Men, this will do the same for the static charge between suit pants and socks.

Slick Trick For Removing Splinters

A drop of vegetable cooking oil or baby oil, gently rubbed in, makes it much easier, when using tweezers, to remove many splinters. Bonus Tip: Never handle chemically-treated wood without wearing thick gloves – the splinters leave painful, infected-like places in the skin. Even though production of this type of wood is now being prohibited by law, there's still a lot of it around, and certainly, never burn treated wood.

Nifty Tips For Removing Glass Ring Stains From Furniture

About every home has one – a small white stain or ring on your wood furniture (these are caused by moisture, like condensation from a cold glass). To remove these stains, use your bare finger or soft cloth to gently rub "ordinary" toothpaste (not the gel type) into the white stain, rubbing with the grain, then carefully dab with a wet cloth to wipe clean. Repeat as needed. You may need to touch up with some mineral or linseed oil, which can then be sealed in by buffing in some furniture paste. Another good remedy is to thickly coat the stain with petroleum jelly, leaving it there for 2 full days – often the petroleum jelly will absorb into the white stain, and blend out the wood color. If this doesn't work, gently rub (with the grain!) the white stain with mineral spirits, using #0000 steel wool. Touch up with stain, or shoe polish, if needed, and polish with a soft cloth.

How To Repair Cracks In A Window

If you have a small crack in a windowpane, don't replace or ignore it. Instead, place a drop or two of super glue (the thin-mixture type) on the center of the crack – "capillary" flow will usually pull the glue throughout the entire crack. This not only seals the crack reducing energy loss and the chance of complete breakage, but will often make the crack disappear. A hypodermic needle filled with thin super glue, or a windshield repair kit, also work well for this repair.

What You Don't Know About Rhubarb . . .

Rhubarb pie is one of the great Southern deserts, although it doesn't seem to be as poplar as it was 30 years ago, when it seemed most folks had a patch of rhubarb in their yard or garden. The rhubarb stalk cooked in a pie is a real treat. However, there are two important things not widely known about this plant: 1. When raising rhubarb, don't let it develop flowers (clip' um!), because these blooms cut back the new stalks in next year's crop. 2. Rhubarb **LEAVES** (not the edible stalk) are poisonous!

Use "Rice" To Relieve Sprains

Soft tissue injuries – like minor sprains, strains, bumps and bruises – are very common. Proper treatment can cut recovery time for the injury in half. For these situations, remember the code word "RICE", which means: 1. **Rest** the injured limb. 2. Apply **Ice** in 15-20 minute-long intervals, every half hour, for the first four to six hours after the injury to reduce swelling. Don't overdo it – never apply ice longer than 20 minutes at a time 3. Use **Compression** on the injury, by intermittingly wrapping it with an elastic bandage (release compression regularly to maintain good circulation). 4. **Elevate** the injured area to a height higher than your heart if possible. Remember to stay away from using intermittent heat for at least 48 hours, and then, not until swelling has subsided and the injury is beginning to heal. Heat increases blood flow and healing, but also causes swelling. Five to ten minutes of heat, at a time, should be plenty. See your physician, of course, for more serious injuries.

The Secret For Getting Rid Of "Ring Around The Collar"

To remove "ring around the collar", soak the shirt collar with your shampoo (squeeze bottle works best for this – no conditioner!). Let it soak about 30 minutes and then run through your regular wash cycle. Collar's clean! After all, shampoo is designed to remove body oils.

Sweet Scheme For Ripening Green Tomatoes

Place green tomatoes in the styrofoam cooler left over from your last picnic, and add an apple or two in there, along with the tomatoes. This really speeds up the ripening process. Bonus Tip: A few apples stored in with your crate or sack of potatoes, will slow down the sprouting of the potatoes.

Keep Rubber Seals On Car Doors & Trunk Lid From Sticking & Cracking

Rub vegetable-based cooking oil or use a non-stick food spray on rubber seals that edge the door and trunk openings of your car or truck, using a generous application when they begin to dry out and crack, or begin to stick from summer heat (especially the trunk lid which is less frequently opened). This works especially well on the rubber door and trunk lid seals of older model vehicles. The food oil or spray won't deteriorate the rubber like oil-based lubricants can.

Surprise Ruler In Your Pocket

Remember that a dollar bill and other U.S. paper currency is just barely over 6 inches in length about (6-1/8" to be more exact), and slightly more than 2-1/2 inches in width. This can be a handy measuring tool.

Sure-Fire Way To "Prime" A Cast Iron Skillet

Some old recipes, like cornbread, taste their best only when cooked in cast iron skillet. Old timers would, ever so often, place their cast iron skillet in a fire to "burn off" the build up of grease and food flavors permeated into their skillet, and then rub down their skillet with lard to keep it from rusting. As a more modern approach, thoroughly scrub and dry your cast iron skillet. Next, really heat it up on the stove. Before storing the skillet and after it cools, spray it with a non-stick food spray, or rub it down with Crisco or vegetable oil, to prevent rusting and get it ready for the next round of "sweetmilk" cornbread. To keep a new skillet from giving your first meal cooked in it that "cast iron" taste, rub it with vegetable oil and really heat it up. Remember – don't stick your cast iron skillet in cold water, to quickly cool it off – you'll permanent warp your skillet! Bonus Tip: If you are left with a skillet or pan containing a layer of burned food, soak a cloth or three-layered paper towel in ammonia, lay the cloth or triple-layered paper towel directly on the burned area, and seal it overnight in an airtight plastic bag. Next day, the clean-up job will be remarkably easier.

Clean And Effective Tag-Team To Sanitize Cutting Boards

Keep a small spray bottle of white vinegar, and a small spray bottle of hydrogen peroxide, in your kitchen cabinet near the cutting board. To clean and disinfect your plastic or wood cutting board, first spray it with a mist of vinegar, and next with a mist of peroxide. Let this mixture stay on a few minutes, for maximum effort. This inexpensive team of household products kills bacteria, and will not harm or even affect the taste of the next line-up of produce or meat placed on the cutting board. Even pure bleach is not as effective on wood cutting boards as this combo of vinegar and peroxide, because wood, by its own natural composition, neutralizes the germ-killing qualities of bleach. Bonus Tip: Microwaving a plastic cutting board does not get it hot enough to disinfect it.

Protect Your Photos With Acid-Free Paper

When you purchase frames to display your favorite photographs, remember that the piece of cardboard that provides the support-backing for the inserted photo, is almost always a highly acidic cardboard that will eventually ruin the photo. You can pick up a large sheet of "acid-free" mat board at your local frame shop, quite inexpensively, and frame many photos with it. This simple step will protect and preserve your special memories.

Easy Way To Sanitize Toothbrushes

Stick your toothbrushes in the silverware rack of the dishwasher, next time you run a load – they'll come out clean, fresh and sanitized. Since dishwashers are operated daily, this is a routine and effective way, when there are children in the family, to keep down colds and sickness that can be passed around by accidental sharing of toothbrushes.

FOUR MOST IMPORTANT WORDS WHEN SAVING A DROWNING VICTIM

In the first day of my lifeguard training as a young Boy Scout, my instructor reminded us that the rescuers themselves often drown in those frantic moments trying to save others in a pool or lake, and that it is vitally important the rescuer remember how to choose the safest method to save the drowning victim. He drove this lesson home with these four words, which I never forgot. (1) REACH. First, "reach" for them from a dock, shore or boat with a pole, broom or other object. Reaching by pole is safer than by hand-to-hand, because a drowning person, in panic, can easily pull in a stronger non-swimmer. (2) THROW. Next, if "reach" is not possible, throw a ring buoy, rope or floating device to the drowning person. (3) ROW. If there is nothing to "throw", then "row" or take your boat out to assist the drowning person. (4) GO. Going after the person by swimming to save them, is the last resort and most dangerous part of the rescue. REACH – THROW – ROW – GO. Not only an easy-to-remember rescue guide, but also reminds us of the importance keeping safety gear like reach poles, ring buoys and other rescue devices around our pool, boat or lake, so that we never have to "GO".

A Handy Way To Seal Storage Boxes

Next time you're sealing up storage boxes with shipping or other tape, try this handy little trick. Before applying the tape over the lid section of the box, lay a string across the same route where the tape will go. Then apply the tape on top of and centering the string, leaving 4-5 inches of string hanging out from one end of the tape. When you get ready to open the box next season, rather than face the aggravation of scraping up the edges of sealed tape or using a box knife, just pull the string and peel off the tape!

Secrets To Attract Fish And Catch Trout By Hand

Rig up a piece of aluminum foil, so that it spins and dangles just over the top of the water, in a good fish habitat area. Quietly slip back to this fishing spot in a few hours during prime fishing time – the bass will be hanging around, waiting on your hook! By the way, if you can reach under a trout with your hand on the edge of a stream or rock, slowly tickle his stomach – the trout will remain perfectly still, and you can grab him with the other hand. Works on catfish too. Don't laugh—the Native Americans caught fish by hand for centuries.

How To Separate Water Out Of Gasoline

If someone on your boat trip leaves the top off the gas can and it rains in it, it can be real trouble. Or you let water get in the gasoline can for your lawnmower. Don't panic. Pour the water-contaminated gasoline through a piece of **canvas,** from a tent, tarp or canopy – the gas will pour through the canvas, but most of the water won't.

Restore Shine To Household Plants With "Mayo" Clinic

To restore a healthy shine to the leaves on household plants, rub mayonnaise on the slick, shiny side of each leaf, and wipe off the excess. Bonus Tip: If you need to extend the length of stems of flowers after several trimmings or for a deeper vase, stick them in soda straws!

Easy Test To Know If Shower Is Wasting Water

Fill a waxed juice or milk carton (1/2 gallon size) to the half-way point with water, and set it under the shower spray. If the carton fills up in less than 12 seconds, your shower is wasting water and overworking your water heater. You can inexpensively purchase and install a low-flow showerhead, or an aerating "massage" attachment, that will save lots of money on both your water and utility bills, and extend the life of your water heater. By the way, did you know a 5 minute shower uses 50% less water than the typical bath? Did you know that you use an extra 2-3 gallons of water when you brush your teeth or shave, and leave the water running? Bonus Tip: To get the jump on cleaning your shower, first close the curtain or shower door, and let scalding hot water run for about 5 minutes. The steam will loosen the build-up of soap film and grime, making the cleaning job much, much easier.

Get Rid Of Pesky Slugs

Gardens, landscaped areas and flowerbeds with shaded, damp soil are prime slug territory. To make homemade slug traps, fill jar lids with beer, and place them around the slug's favorite plants. The slugs will crawl in and drown. Remove the slugs each day, as you refill the lids.

How To Get Loose From A Snapping Turtle – Before It Thunders

It has long been a mountain legend, that if a snapping turtle bites you it won't let go "until it thunders". In reality, the vicious bite of a snapping turtle can take off a finger, and their claws cut to the bone. If you're unlucky enough to be bitten by a snapping turtle on a cloudless day, there's still hope. Immediately and forcefully shove the turtle's head back into its shell with your foot, or any other way you are instantly able to cram his head back in the shell—and he'll immediately let go. Another method of escape is to cram a stick or sharp object in the turtle's nostril—he'll let go.

What To Do If Lost In The Snow

Years ago, I learned about a survival tip that can save a hunter or hiker's life, or anyone else, if lost in very cold, snowy weather, where a person can greatly increase their danger by aimlessly trudging through snow, burning up a limited supply of energy and stop to rest only at the risk of going to sleep and freezing to death. If a lost person is unable to build a fire, find or build any shelter or reach assistance, one survival option is to walk, in a very slow, deliberate and steady fashion, around and around a tree. This slow walk helps to keep the body warm, the mind clear, and soon wears away the snow around the tree so walking becomes effortless and uses very little of your precious energy, until help arrives.

Good But Little-Known Remedy For A Minor Sore Throat

This remedy comes from a physician, who let me in on the secret. When suffering a minor and routine sore throat, take a healthy "swig" of Listerine, and lean your head back so that the mouthwash fills and lies still in the throat for two full minutes, before spitting it out. Don't gargle! Repeat this procedure 5-6 times per day, until the sore throat is gone. Of course, if the sore throat doesn't improve in the next day or two, see your physician immediately.

Secrets To Keeping Fresh Cheese On The Trail

If you're going hiking or camping for a few days and won't have access to a cooler, you can still enjoy fresh cheese by first wrapping it in 3-4 layers of fresh cabbage leaves, next wrapping the cheese and cabbage leaves with cellophane wrap, and then packing it in a seal-up plastic baggie. Speaking of cabbage, the mothers of farm families and long-time gardeners will tell you that cabbage keeps best, if placed in the refrigerator or in a cool basement, without washing or unwrapping it. Bonus Tip: At home, you can keep cheese from getting moldy in your refrigerator by placing it in an air-tight container along with 2 or 3 lumps of sugar.

How To Avoid Clogged Spray Cans

Hairspray. Paint. Deodorant. All spray cans will clog up. There's a simple trick to prevent a clogged can. How? Simply turn the can upside down, and give it a brief spray – this will clear the nozzle for the next use. If already clogged, first try this upside down spray method, and if still clogged, wipe the nozzle with mineral spirits or fingernail polish remover. If super-clogged, you can either shoot a burst of spray lubricant (like WD-40) through its straw-shaped spray tube into the bottom of the nozzle to clear it out, or you can remove and soak the nozzle in mineral spirits overnight; this always clear the toughest clogs. Bonus Tip: Save a nozzle or two from empty cans of products you regularly use and place them in zip-seal plastic bag – they'll come in handy next time you have a tough clog, or a defective nozzle.

Remember The "Three Easy S's" To Remove Most Stains

Professional cleansers privately tell me that although some stains require special chemicals and treatment (such as motor oil, enamel, paint, ink, tree sap), that most other common stains from blood, catsup, chocolate, coffee, tea, fruit juice, milk, mustard, soft drinks, mayo and salad dressing, can be successfully removed at home, *if you act very quickly*, by following the three easy "S's". That is, **Soak** the stain in cold water; **Saturate** the stain with liquid laundry detergent; **Scrub** the stain by running it through the washer. Here's a little more details about the three easy S's: (1) For the **soak** step, place the stained material in cold water for 30 minutes (before soaking, gently scrap off any excess stain with a plastic spoon or dull knife); (2) For the **saturate** step, rub good quality liquid laundry detergent (which is, by the way, scientifically developed to loosen dirt and stains) deeply into the stain while still wet, and let it soak at least 30 minutes. Rinse with cold water and for especially stubborn stains, repeat this process along with some dabbing, rubbing or brushing of the stain with the detergent, to the extent the material will stand without being damaged; and (3) For the **scrub** step, run through the regular wash cycle, using warm water. Remember, hot water locks in stains. Attacking stains immediately is the key, because the faster you respond to remove the stain – the better the results. Bleach can help with solid whites. Brush stains from their outer edges to their center, to avoid spreading the stain. Bonus Tip: If you can't get to this stain removal process until the next day or so, wet the stained area and place the cloth item in a sealed-off plastic bag, and stuff it in the freezer until you're ready.

TACTICS FOR YOUR TOOL BOX

Tool boxes trap moisture, and can rust your tools left inside. Also, tools get scratched, as they toss around when the tool box is moved, rubbing against each other and the bottom of the metal tool box. There's a simple cure. Place a charcoal briquette in your tool box, to absorb moisture; occasionally heat it up in your oven, to rid it of built-up moisture. Cut a piece of discarded carpet for the bottom of your tool box, which will minimize damage to your tools, and "quieten" the tool box. Bonus Tip: Keep a "bobby pin" in your tool box—they work great, for holding and hammering tacks or nails that are too small to hold with your fingers.

Treatment For Stinky Shoes

To freshen up sweaty or sour shoes, sift the insides with a coating of baking soda, then shake up the shoes thoroughly. The next day, empty out the baking soda. Presto – fresh shoes! Bonus Tip: To avoid the "shake-out" of loose baking soda, tie it off in two cotton rags, and then stuff one in each shoe to deodorize.

Nice Tip For Stirring Paint With A Stick

A paint stick, used to stir paint, is twice as effective, if you drill several pencil-size holes in its length. With each stir stroke, the paint flows in and out of the holes resulting in faster and better mixing. Rinse the stick after stirring, so holes won't clog up. Bonus Tip: When taking on a pretty big painting job at home, pull a pair of old cotton athletic socks over your shoes, to keep them splatter free.

How To Make Super-Strong Storage Case For Long Objects

If you need a strong protective case, especially for long and narrow objects like a cue stick, fishing rod, rare walking cane, or set of blueprints, make one yourself as follows: Purchase a section of "PVC" tubing (it's a durable and long-lasting plastic pipe) at your local building-supply or hardware store, selecting the length and width you need for your particular object. Also purchase one "end cap", one "screw cap" and a can of PVC cement. Glue on the "end cap", as the permanently-closed end of the case. Then glue on the "screw cap" that comes in two pieces (one piece, called the screw base, is to be glued on; the other end screws on to that base). You now have a permanent and crush-proof case, ready for travel or storage!

A "Bottom"-Line Tip About Cane-Bottom Chairs

One of the most treasured pieces I have, is a wooden clothes valet shaped into a cane-bottom chair, made and woven by my father in his workshop. Many people treasure their cane-bottom chairs and rockers, because hand-woven cane bottoms are always a labor of love, patience and craftsmanship. The tip? Leave the cane unfinished and natural if possible, and avoid varnishing or shellacking it. The varnish, laquer or shellac will dry out the cane, and significantly weaken it. Bonus Tip: When preparing to apply laquer with a brush, don't shake it up or even stir it—you'll create air bubbles, that will show up on the surface of the piece you are coating.

Storing And Keeping Paint Brushes Soft Is A Zip

Store cleaned paint brushes in zip-seal plastic bags, and add a dab of liquid fabric softener in the plastic bag, or wrap the brush in a sheet of fabric softener and place it in the bag – this will keep bristles soft. Bonus Tip: For small touch-up or detailed jobs, use cotton swabs as brushes to apply paint. Place paint in a paper cup, for easy use of the swabs. Another Bonus Tip: To soften up rock-hard paint brushes, soak them in a mixture of ½ quart of kerosene, ½ quart of warm water and 4 tablespoons of salt.

How To Get The Tick Off; Not Ticked Off

Ticks are a way of life in the mountains of Appalachia. Home remedies have been passed around for centuries, on how best to remove a tick from the skin. Old timers "dowsed" the tick in a fuel called "coal oil", or pulled them off by grabbing the tick between their thumb and knife blade. Some folks suffocate the tick with petroleum jelly before removing it. Others, still today, stick the head of a hot, blown-out match to the tick, hoping to encourage its departure. Despite these home remedies, the safest way to remove a tick – is the most simple. Grab the tick with tweezers (hold firmly, but don't crush the tick!), if possible, right behind its mouth where it has bitten into the skin. Then, slowly and firmly pull the tick off. Don't try to suddenly yank the tick off! Remember, if you "smash" the tick with the tweezers, you are literally forcing tick bacteria into your system. Lastly, give the bite a good soapy wash, and apply anti-bacterial ointment.

Best Homemade Antidote For Skunk Spray

Peppy Les Peu is a pretty funny cartoon character, but getting sprayed by a skunk is no laughing matter. It really happens. Most often, it's pets, not people who get perfumed. Early frontiersmen would build a fire, and hold their clothing over cedar smoke. Many people still believe in washing down with tomato juice. The best home remedy, according to Appalachian folks in my area, is the following recipe for skunk odor de-bunker: mix together one quart of hydrogen peroxide, one-fourth cup of dishwashing liquid and one-half cup of baking soda. Scrub down with this concoction, rinse, and then take a good, long soak with the other half-box of baking soda dissolved in the bath water. By the way, this "skunk scrub" works well for pets.

Secret To Keeping Vegetables Fresh In The Fridge

You can keep your vegetables fresh and crisp in your refrigerator, for a longer period of time, as follows: First place several sheets of black and white newspaper (like the size of sports section) in the bottom of your vegetable bin. Next, place a few more layers of paper towels on top of the newspaper. This "vegetable pad" will absorb the moisture that quickly ruins and shortens the useable life of your vegetables. Bonus Tip: If you're going to use only one-half of an onion, use the top half. The bottom half of an onion contains the root, and will last longer!

A Nifty Trick For Planting Straight Rows

To keep the rows straight when you plant in your flower or victory garden make a "row plumb" as follows: Fill two 1-gallon plastic milk jugs with water, cut a string the length of the rows you are planting and tie the string between the handles of these jugs. Now you can stretch out the jugs on the ground as a straight-line guide for planting your garden rows, without the hassle of the usual method of driving and removing string-and-stakes from row to row.

Fast & Easy Solution For Stuck Zippers

Spray a quick shot of non-stick food spray in a stuck zipper to work it loose – this vegetable-based lubricant won't damage clothing or give off an oily smell, like oil based lubricants. Or, you can rub soap in the stuck zipper mechanism to work it loose, and on the full length of the zipper itself to keep it working smoothly.

HOME REMEDY RELIEF FROM SUNBURN AND CHIGGERS

Being covered with chigger or seed tick bites is pretty miserable – all you want to do is scratch. To get some soothing relief from chiggers, mosquito, or other multiple insect bites, or even from minor sunburn, sprinkle a generous amount of baking soda in a warm tub of water, and take a good long soak. You'll feel better.

Don't Backstroke From Swimmer's Ear – There's A Homemade Remedy

For "swimmer's ear", or if feeling the early onset of mild ear infection, to make your own solution to irrigate the ear, mix together in a sterile container equal portions of rubbing alcohol and white vinegar. With an eyedropper, place a few drops into the ear canal, and then turn the head downward to allow the solution to run back out. This procedure can also be a good preventive measure, if the children are swimming at the lake or pool every day, but don't use it if the person's eardrum has ever been perforated by injury or infection. Of course, if the mild ear infection does not promptly improve and go away, immediately consult with your physician.

Table Sugar Can Speed-Up Healing Of Minor Cuts And Burns

Table sugar (not brown or powdered sugar) can often accelerate the healing of minor burns, abrasions and cuts, and with less scarring and scabbing. To best use sugar this way, mix together a salve of (a) 4 parts of sugar, and (b) 1 part of an anti-bacterial ointment. After making certain that the bleeding has stopped (sugar can stimulate bleeding) and the injured area is clean, apply this salve mixture, covering with a sterile bandage, and do so 3-4 times a day, rinsing the injured area with hydrogen peroxide before each application.

Seamstress' Secret To Easy Threading Of A Needle

Spray hairspray on your thumb and finger, and roll the end of your thread between them – the thread will stiffen up and be easy to place in the needle. Bonus Tip: When threading a needle, hold the thread stationary between your thumb and finger, and bring the needle to the thread – this is much easier than bringing the thread towards the stationary needle. Another Bonus Tip: If you stick your needle through a "fabric softener" sheet, three or four times, your needle will pierce through the cloth or other fabric, much easier! However, make sure that you thread the needle and tie a knot in the thread, before you use this technique.

A DANGEROUS MYTH ABOUT TIRES

It has long been a custom and commonly believed, that a person can let air out of their car tires to "get more tire in contact with the road" and thus "more traction". Experts say this is a terrible idea that doesn't work and is very dangerous. Underinflated tires wear out faster and cut down fuel efficiency at least 5%. Always carefully follow the manufacturer's recommendations for the amount of air in your tires. Bonus Tip: The most accurate and reliable time to check tire pressure is before your drive, while they are still cool.

Some Amazing Uses Of Toothpaste – That May Surprise You

1. To remove or reduce a scratch on glass or a mirror, slowly and gently rub "ordinary" toothpaste (not the gel type) on the scratch, using your finger covered with a soft cotton cloth. Check your progress by dabbing the spot clean with a water-soaked paper towel. Dry and repeat as needed. 2. Generously apply ordinary toothpaste (again, not the gel type) to pimples on your face when you get home. Next morning, they'll be much improved. 3. Ordinary toothpaste placed on a soft cotton cloth, can be used to carefully rub and remove crayon marks from painted sheetrock or plaster walls. 4. A good hand scrub with ordinary toothpaste, will remove the "fish" smell left over from your fishing trip, or from making salmon patties in the kitchen.

How To Remove Stubborn Tree Sap From Clothes

To remove pine resin or tree sap from clothes, mineral spirits is one of the few things that will actually work. First, scrape off as much resin as possible (a plastic spoon won't damage clothes). Then soak the spot with mineral spirits for about 15 minutes, and dab out as much resin as possible. Next, fill your washer and add ½ cup automatic dishwashing detergent and ½ cup of clothes detergent, allowing the clothing to soak overnight. Next day, run the washer through its cycle.

How To Easily Unclog Your Showerhead Nozzle

To clean out and unclog your showerhead nozzle without the hassle of removing it, fill a portion of a strong trash bag with warm white vinegar, placing it over the showerhead so the nozzle is completely immersed. Tightly tie off the bag just above the nozzle head. Let the nozzle soak about 12 hours and remove it. All clear!

SENSATIONAL TIP FOR UNTANGLING KNOTTED JEWELRY CHAINS

To untangle jewelry chains that are knotted up, lay the chain on waxed paper, generously spray the knotted area with a non-stick food spray or place a drop of vegetable cooking oil on the knot. Then loosen the knot with straight pins, and untangle. Simply rinse off the food spray or cooking oil with warm water.

Use A Potato To Safely Remove A Broken Bulb

To remove a light bulb that is broken-off in its socket, first make sure the power cord is unplugged. Next use the tool of choice for this job, which is needle-nose pliers, to remove the bulb socket. However, if you don't have needle-nose pliers, carefully push a potato down on the socket of the broken bulb so that it sticks on the remaining glass shards, then simply twist out the bulb socket.

Hosiery As Vacuum Accessory For Small And Delicate Items

When you need to vacuum fur-covered game trophies, delicate cloth items or your computer keyboard, all without risk of harming them (or sucking the keys off of your keypad), do this—slip panty hose or a nylon stocking over the vacuum nozzle, stretch a rubber band tightly around the hosiery just below the nozzle opening, and vacuum away. However, when possible suction without making contact—its best not to push the vac nozzle up against the delicate trophy or cloth item being cleaned. A feather duster, sprayed with Endust or similar product and left overnight in a sealed plastic bag, works well on mounted birds and fish. Bonus Tip: This vacuum method is a great way to find precious stones (broken loose from their jewelry setting), earrings, tiny screws or parts, contact lens or any other very small items lost in the carpet or furniture – these items, when suctioned, will safely cling to the mesh covering provided by the hosiery.

How The "Pause" Mode Can Damage Your VCR Or Camcorder

When you take an intermission at home from watching a movie or home video to answer a telephone call or eat supper, don't leave your VCR in the "pause" mode. Why? While locked in the "pause" mode, most VCR and camcorder heads are still spinning against this one same spot on the stopped or "paused" video tape. This can rub a chemical off of the tape and leave it behind as a residue on the heads, eventually causing the heads to jam-up or malfunction. Bonus Tip: If you rarely use your VCR, at least once a month, put in a tape and run it both ways by fast-forwarding it to the end, and then fast-reversing it back to the beginning. This will keep the VCR bearings greased, and prevent the lubricant from drying up as a result of non-use.

Keep Away Venomous Snakes

It is still believed by folks in rural areas, that you can keep away rattlesnakes, copperheads and other snakes away from under your storage buildings, farm sheds and wood piles, by generously sprinkling moth balls or moth crystals under the building. There is strong anecdotal evidence that this truly works – but not directly on the snakes. The moth balls repel mice and other varmints in the snake's food chain – so there's no reason for snakes to hang around. Remember – moth balls are poisonous, so make sure that young children cannot access them.

SECRET TO KEEPING YOUR VAC ON TRACK

Sooner or later, vacuuming up small metal things, like bobby pins, screws and paper clips, will damage your vacuum cleaner. A gentleman who had maintained and vacuumed church and school floors for decades gave me this good piece of advice. Here it is. A strong magnet strip, fastened across and hanging down from the front edge of the suction head of an upright vacuum cleaner, will grab most of these small metal objects before they are pulled into the vacuum and damage the vac motor or the fan that creates the suction. You can rig your own, but the easiest solution is to check out the web site www.janitorialsupplies.com where you can find these specialty magnets, made just for this purpose, for only a few dollars.

Vinegar As Homemade Remedy To Relieve Minor Fungal Rashes And Oily Hair

Vinegar can often work as a simple and effective treatment for mild fungal infections, such as athlete's foot, scalp irritations or jock itch. With a sterile cotton ball or clean cotton cloth, apply white vinegar to the area 2-3 times a day, or soak and rinse your hair once a day after shampooing (this also restores hair to its correct pH), until itching disappears, and then continue for about 5 days thereafter. If the rash becomes severe, gets infected, or fails to promptly clear up, immediately see your physician. To dry off after treating feet or jock itch, use a hair dryer, which works much better than a towel. To get rid of oily hair, mix a tablespoon of white vinegar with a quart of water, and use, after shampooing, as a final rinse.

Use A Penny To Check Tire Treads

To quick-check your tire treads, you need only borrow a penny. Stick a penny down into a groove on your tire, so that the top of Abraham Lincoln's head is pointing downward into the groove. The test: if the top of Lincoln's head shows, there is very little tread left and the tire should be replaced. If the top of Lincoln's head extends down into the groove and out of view, the tire treads still have more miles left on them. However, this is only a fast, on-the-spot method for checking tire tread, and should not be relied upon as the final word on tire condition.

Avoid Damage By Putting Pads On Wall Hangings

When you hang your photos, art or other framed pictures on the wall, invest in a $1.00 pack of framing pads. These pads are each a little smaller than a dime, and stick on the back of the framed picture at its four corners. These pads protect the wall from being scuffed, make small adjustments possible in leveling the frame, and allow air to circulate behind the frame preventing discoloration of the wall. Adhesive-backed floor protectors (they can be cut into halves or fourths to extend their use), used on the bottom on furniture legs to protect floors, are excelled for this use, since they're a little thicker, and work well for heavier wall hangings (mirrors, large frames, etc.).

How To Keep Wasps And Hornets From Ruining Your Day

If wasps are crowding in on you while relaxing outside on your porch or deck, try this diversion: Pour about three inches of apple cider vinegar in a long neck bottle, or if need be a more decorative container, and set it up on a high ledge or other place conspicuous to the wasps, but away from your area of relaxation. The vinegar should draw them to the bottle, and away from you. If you are at a picnic site near a lake or camping, and find yourself being tormented by hornets, try this fisherman's method of getting some relief: Hang a dead fish, the larger the better (hang it by a string tied around the tail fin), only 1-2 inches over the surface of the water, or hang the fish in the same manner over a bucket of water, which you should place in a spot close enough to catch the hornets' attention but far enough away from you to give you some peace. The hornets will feed and gorge themselves on the fish, and drop off into the water because their too full to fly.

Lost? Use Your Watch As A Compass

If you are ever lost without a compass, this little trick could be of great help to you. Hold your watch so it is face up and parallel to the ground. Turn your watch face so that the hour hand is pointing directly towards the sun. Find the point on your watch, using the shorter arc, which is exactly **halfway** between the hour hand (which is pointing towards the sun) and the 12 o'clock point on your watch—this "halfway" point will be SOUTH. Make sure your watch is correctly set for the standard time in the area you are located. For example, if this technique is properly done at 8:00 a.m., then the "midway" line drawn from the center of your watch (which will lie midway between the hour hand pointing at 8:00 o'clock and the sun and the 12:00 o'clock digits on your watch) will pass outward through the 10:00 o'clock digits and thus be pointing toward the true south—meaning true north is in the opposite direction of the 4:00 o'clock digits on your watch. To be more accurate in lining up with the sun, you can hold a pine needle, toothpick or thin twig upright at the edge of your watch, like a sundial, to form a shadow that aligns with the hour hand. Practice this technique, checking yourself with a compass. If the sun is not visible and totally blocked by the clouds, don't panic. Again, hold a pine needle or toothpick in an upright fashion at a 90 degree angle on white paper. The sun will cast a faint shadow on the paper revealing the position of the sun to you, then allowing you to align the hour hand of your watch with the sun.

HOW TO SAVE A WATERLOGGED BOOK

If you ever drop or soak a book in water, before throwing it away or leaving it to warp in a slow drying process, try this amazing remedy: put the book in a **frost-free** freezer for a few hours. The freezer will draw out all of the moisture, and even allow you to separate the pages. You can also sift baby or talcum powder between the pages of a damp book, brush out the powder several hours later, and get good drying results.

Curing A Troublesome Wheelbarrow Tire

The tires on new and used wheelbarrows, especially during heavy-load use, are usually low on air, leaky and a real hassle to pump up, remove or haul to the service station for air. Fill your low wheelbarrow tire with a can of a "stop-leak" type product, commonly used for emergency flat tires on your car. This will likely eliminate your wheelbarrow tire problems.

How To Get The Juice, Loose

Many folks enjoy a glass of fresh-squeezed orange juice in the morning. Electric juicers have made this treat more popular. So will this nifty trick. Before juicing the oranges, which are often kept in the refrigerator, place the ones to be juiced in a large bowl of hot water, and leave them there in their own hot tub for 15-20 minutes. Result? They'll juice "easier" and juice "more". Works great for lemons too. Bonus Tip: There's a quick and easy way to peel peaches, tomatoes, and other soft-skin fruit and vegetables. Drop the fruit or vegetable in boiling water for a few seconds, and then place it in cold water—the skin will come off, quick and easy!

How To Make Great Windshield Washer Fluid

Mix 3 parts of white vinegar to 1 part water. This formula won't freeze in its container, and only costs pennies! Bonus Tip: Want to know a convenient way to store a heavy-duty set of jumper cables in your vehicle. Of course, the problem is that jumper cables spread out in the trunk, bang around, constantly get in the way, and never easily fit back into the carrier pouch they come in. Here's a good solution given to me by a friend. Get a 3 or 5 gallon plastic bucket (depending on the size of the jumper cables) with a pop-on lid, available at most building supply stores. The jumper cables will coil up and store nicely inside, and the bucket tucks away nicely inside the trunk.

Avoid Storing Videos Too Close To TV

It's mighty handy to keep videos right next to the TV and VCR – but be careful. Television sets give off a pretty strong magnetic field that can sometimes damage video tapes, if they're stored too close for too long. Remember, to further extend the life of video tapes, stack them vertically on their narrow ends like you would books and not on their broad sides, which allows video tape to sag and ruin.

The Secret To A Super-Strong Installation Of A Post In The Ground

While building a set of handrails along a wooded walking trail behind my home, I ran smack dab into a problem – how to install wooden posts in the ground, so they'll stay firm in place. Eventually, most wood or metal posts placed in the ground (unless they have a "truckload" of cement poured around them), begin to shift and loosen. Here's a "rock-solid" solution. After the hole for your post is dug out, reach down in the hole and drive four or five pieces of angle iron (also called "rebar") horizontally into the ground, at slightly downward angles; do this in the bottom section of the hole that will be filled with cement. These pieces of rebar should be about 2-1/2 – 3 ft. in length. Drive each piece of angle iron snugly into the ground, so that 2-3 inches of the rebar is extending out of the ground into the hole. Leave just enough room to drop your post down the center of the hole, so it is nestled inside the tripod-like ring of angle iron pieces. When you pour cement into the hole, it will adhere both to the rebar and the post, for a super-strong installation. This method works great for wood and metal posts, and for clothes lines, purple martin houses, gateposts and flagpoles.

A Simple Way To Extend The Life Of Your Zippers

Always zip up your jackets, pants and other clothing containing zippers, before washing and drying them. Washers and dryers are hard on zipper teeth banging them out of alignment, later causing them to hang or jam-up during use. Zipping up before tossing them in the washer and dryer, protects the zipper teeth and extends the workable life of the zipper.

A Reliable Roadmap For Buying A Used Car – To Avoid A "Wreck"

Buying a used car can be a great way to afford a good, solid vehicle – or it can be a financial disaster. Here is my roadmap to guide the potential buyers of used cars, that will reduce the chances of such a disaster – a roadmap drawn upon my experience of hearing hundreds of court cases and listening to the testimony of certified mechanics and automotive experts: 1. Have a reputable mechanic or engine specialist check a critically-important thing called "**compression**", and explain the results to you; 2. Have the **alignment** checked, looking for signs of past accidents and chassis damage; 3. Check for *leaks* under the car engine area, by letting the car engine run for about 15 minutes while parked over newspapers; 4. Ask the dealer to promise to you **in writing** that the **odometer reading** is accurate and that the car has not been exposed to flood damage, or been reconstructed or salvaged from a previous wreck. *Some Warning Signs:* (a) Weird sounds coming from the engine; (b) Fresh leaks under the car; (c) Warning lights or dash indicators coming on; (d) Spliced wires in the trunk; (e) Electrical problems or lights not working; (f) Different color paint or welding signs inside the door jams, or color variation or paint splash inside the gas cap area; (g) Fresh paint job on an old car (wrecked cars are almost always re-painted; "re-paints" almost always show up inside the gas cap door). *Some Recommendations:* 1. Find out if the air bag has been deployed (if so, it's very costly to replace and a sure sign of previous wreck); 2. Avoid and be careful buying at auction (lack of reliable information about the car and no legal recourse if you get a lemon) or when a vehicle has been repeatedly sold and shifted around among used car dealers; 3. Search for cars sold by dealers who serviced them (that is, try to buy a Ford from a Ford dealer); 4. Insist upon seeing the service records when possible, and the name/address of previous owners (call the previous owners to discuss the car's mileage, repair record and performance history). 5. Odometer tampering goes on everywhere; be suspicious of worn-looking cars with surprisingly low mileage. Compare dates and corresponding mileages on services records, or mileage information given to you by the prior owner, to warn for the possibility of odometer rollback; 5. Check the rating of the car in Consumer Report's "Buyer's Guide" (they identify the most reliable used cars with a good repair record, and those with a bad track record); and 7. Get the VIN number on the car, and for a small charge, run it through "Carfax" service either at 1-800-346-3846 or on-line to get a complete title history on the car, which can, among other valuable information, sometimes reveal "reconstructed" or "salvage" titles from wrecked vehicles, flood damage and dealer "buy-back" of lemons . Finally, keep on alert for "certified" used cars (the extra cost is usually well worth it), one-owner vehicles (easier to get complete service records and performance history), and for used cars with significant warranty coverage remaining (however—find out how much warranty time is actually left, and know what is *not* covered by the warranty). **Remember the old adage: "don't fall in love with a car, because they don't love you back".** Do your homework. The buyer's power is in the right to say "no", and walk away from the "greatest deal of a lifetime". If you're not sure, or the dealer discourages you from taking any of the precautions recommended above – just don't buy it . . . there's **always** another car.